Ea

Lothians

HOLY
CORNERS

with best wishes,
Michael Turnbull
30 April 1996

Michael T R B Turnbull

SAINT ANDREW PRESS
EDINBURGH

First published in 1996 by
SAINT ANDREW PRESS
121 George Street, Edinburgh EH2 4YN

Copyright © Michael T R B Turnbull 1996

ISBN 0 7152 0689 3

British Library Cataloguing in Publication Data
A catalogue record for this book
is available from the British Library.

ISBN 0715206893

Etchings are adapted from J Grant: *Old and New Edinburgh* (Cassell, 1887), vol 1; Samuel Green: *Scottish Pictures* (Religious Tract Society, 1891); J A Wylie: *The Scots Worthies* (Wm Mackenzie, 1880); and 'The Scottish Annals' from Macfarlane/Thomson: *The Comprehensive History of England* (Blackie & Sons, 1861).
Cover and **design concept** by Mark Blackadder.
Cover photographs by Walter Bell and Michael Turnbull.
Main cover picture by Walter Bell, taken from the Camera Obscura, Castlehill, Edinburgh.
Typeset in 11/12 pt Garamond by Lesley A Taylor.
Printed and **bound** by Athenaeum Press Ltd, Gateshead, Tyne & Wear.

CONTENTS

For Hester
and for
Tynepark Resource Centre

EDINBURGH *from the* SOUTH, 1650

ACKNOWLEDGMENTS

I would like to thank all the many people who have given so readily of their time and energy to assist me: in particular, those who have shared their views and experience and whose reflections form Part II of this book.

To the dedication and resourcefulness of the librarians at the local history centres in East Lothian, West Lothian, Midlothian and Edinburgh, I owe a special debt.

Lastly, my thanks go to the staff of Saint Andrew Press who have shown me infinite patience, enthusiasm and good humour.

Michael T R B Turnbull
Spring 1996

PART I
The Past

Perhaps it was an early classical education that aroused my interest in gods of places (genius loci); a belated appreciation of William Wordsworth's scenic wonder or memories of Gerald Manley Hopkins' 'inscape' – a revelation of holiness in nature. It was certainly a sense of the religious in the created world that I tried to capture in these pages.

Then there was a more down-to-earth curiosity about the buildings whose public function was religious – Edinburgh's St Giles is the best example, where denominations and varied styles of worship succeeded each other with bewildering speed.

*In **Part I** it is possible to trace a common devotional thread from pre-Reformation to post-Reformation times, in spite of the apparent severity of the disjunction. After all, the great early Reformers did not cease to draw upon their intellectual formation as Roman Catholic clerics, while at the same time rejecting the structures of the Church they left behind.*

Then there was the irrationality and comedy of some aspects of church-going which I felt worth highlighting, such as the three bodies of St Baldred, the verbal subterfuge of ministers in sticky situations and the pantomime antics of churchwardens wounding goats and pigs and cows in the dark, in the mistaken belief that they were grave-robbers!

For readers who stray into the holy corners of Edinburgh and Lothians, the journey is invariably full of fascinating discoveries and stimulating surprises.

Interior *of* St Giles

ONE

EAST LOTHIAN
Pre-Reformation

PRE-HISTORY

East Lothian is not poor in prehistoric sites whose function was predominantly religious. There are burial cairns on Spartleton Edge and Priestlaw Hill and stone circles at the head-waters of the Whiteadder river. On Kingside Hill, thirty small stones surround a low burial mound. There are standing stones at Easter Broomhouse; in a field west of the A1 near Kirklandhill farm (a sandstone pillar nearly three metres high) and on Pencraig Hill.

Among the Roman altars discovered at Inveresk (near Musselburgh) was one dedicated to the god Apollo. Christian burials, laid east to west in stone-lined coffins (*cists*), have come to light at Belhaven, near Dunbar. More explicit Christian symbolism can be seen in three Anglian crosses found at Tyninghame, Morham and Aberlady.

Holy wells existed at Whitekirk, Preston and Stenton. There, the prosperity of the nearby Biel estate was said to depend on the Rood Well (known as the Cardinal's Hat) and, in particular, on the continued sound repair of its roof!

The very earliest Christian missionary settlements were made by St Modwenna (who founded a monastery near Traprain Law around AD 500) and by the omnipresent **ST BALDRED** (*d* 606).

ATHELSTANEFORD
(*known locally as* ELSHINFURD)

The tiny village of Athelstaneford has a unique position in Scottish history as being the place where the Scottish saltire cross (St Andrew's cross) was first seen and adopted as the flag of the Picts and later of Scotland.

Around the year AD 732 the Northumbrian King Athelstane camped here before his battle with the Picts under King Angus mac Fergus.

St Andrew, the future patron saint of Scotland, is said to have appeared to Angus and promised him victory.

During the battle, a huge saltire cross (*crux decussata* – like an 'X') was seen refracted by the rising sun, putting heart into the Picts (rather as one had appeared against the setting sun to the Roman emperor Constantine I before his victory at the Milvian Bridge outside Rome in AD 312).

Athelstane was killed at the ford over the Cogtail burn. From that time on, the Picts carried a white saltire on a blue ground.

DUNBAR

To St Acca (*d* AD 740) and St Wilfrid, Bishop of Hexham (634-709) – who led the Roman faction at the Synod of Whitby in 664 – Dunbar held unpleasant memories, for both of them were imprisoned there.

Wilfrid is said to have brought St Andrew's relics (and those of a number of other saints) back from Rome to Hexham and Acca gave them to Angus mac Fergus, King of the Picts around the time of the battle of Athelstaneford.

Angus wanted to establish St Andrews in Fife as 'the mother of all the churches in the kingdom of the Picts'. Subsequently over the coming centuries, St Andrews would become one of the major pilgrimage centres in Western Europe.

HADDINGTON

Two important religious foundations in Haddington (now both in ruins) were St Martin's Cistercian convent and the Franciscan friary (known as the 'Lamp of Lothian' from its huge glass windows). Nor did the great burgh church of St Mary's escape unscathed from the frequent incursions made by armies from south of the Border. It was badly damaged by English cannon in 1548-49 while harbouring Franco-Scottish sharp-shooters.

Haddington's Grammar School can claim to have educated two outstanding religious figures – the theologian/historian **JOHN MAJOR** (*circa* 1470-1550) and **JOHN KNOX** (*circa* 1513-72), father of the Scottish Reformation.

One apparent miracle is recorded as having taken place in Haddington on the eve of the Nativity of the Virgin (7th September 1358) when the river Tyne, swollen by heavy rain, overflowed its banks, causing widespread damage and loss of life.

ST MARY'S, HADDINGTON – *the unrestored* EAST END

WALTER BOWER (1385-1449), Haddington-born monk and chronicler, relates that when the flood approached the Cistercian convent, one of the nuns took up a small statue of the Virgin Mary and threatened to throw it into the water if the Blessed Virgin did not protect the holy building. Miraculously, the waters of the Tyne subsided.

MUSSELBURGH

The present church of St Michael's, Inveresk is built on the site of a Roman temple dedicated to Jupiter for the use of the nearby Roman fort. In the sixth century St Modwenna built the first Christian church there.

Around 1533, a shrine of Our Lady of Loretto was established at the east side of Musselburgh by Thomas Duthy, a hermit.

Formerly a captain in the Turkish wars, he had brought a statue of the Virgin Mary from Loretto in Italy. As a hermit Duthy granted indulgences and pardon from sin. So revered was the shrine that in 1536 James V made a pilgrimage to it on foot from Stirling Castle.

Since it was believed that pregnant women could have a trouble-free birth if they made an offering at the shrine, about 1558 a Lady Cleishe sent a servant with her shirt and some gold to obtain the grace of an easy delivery.

Among a number of miraculous cures there was a blind man who had apparently regained his sight. Lord Cleishe, who was a Protestant, persuaded him to become his servant and took him home. There he forced him to tell him the truth about his cure. The man revealed how, as a young shepherd boy tending the sheep of the Convent of St Catherine of Siena in Edinburgh, he would play a game by turning his eye-lids over and rolling up the whites of his eyes.

When the nuns had learned of this they sent for a priest who advised the nuns to hide the boy in a cellar for some years till all memory of him had died away.

After eight years he was released by the nuns and then made to pretend to be a blind beggar.

On hearing his story, Lord Cleishe made the boy agree to stand at the Mercat Cross in Edinburgh and reveal his deception. Then he and the boy escaped on horseback to Queens-ferry.

Although the Chapel of Loretto was destroyed by the Earl of Hertford and his army in 1544, it was repaired – but by 1590 it had been largely demolished and the materials used to build the Musselburgh Tolbooth.

Nothing now remains of the chapel except a cell 12 ft x 10 ft, covered by a dome of earth. The school buildings occupying the site of the chapel were constructed in the 1750s.

NORTH BERWICK

St Baldred, a disciple of St Kentigern, lived for a time on the Bass Rock. Two miracle stories are told about him. In the first, a rock (which was a danger to shipping between the Bass Rock and the mainland) floated away to the shore at the word of the holy man and was from that time known as St Baldred's Boat.

In the second story, the villages of Tyning-hame (destroyed AD 941), Auldhame and Prestonkirk all claimed St Baldred's body when he died.

On the advice of a holy man, the disputing parties agreed to pray and sleep on the matter.

The BASS ROCK

The following morning, in each of the three churches, an identical corpse of St Baldred appeared!

There was a convent in North Berwick, founded in 1154 by the Earl of Fife. Originally a Benedictine house, it later became Cistercian. It had a dovecot which could hold 1320 pigeons. Fine pottery tiles were manufactured at the convent in four tile kilns. The nuns were also involved in agriculture (using a sea-weed fertiliser), in milling grain and in wool production.

In 1375 the Pope ordered the Bishop of St Andrews to wall off the North Berwick convent, as the nuns were being molested by noblemen and other secular persons.

Not all the vicars of North Berwick parish church were above reproach. In 1279, for example, David the vicar was arrested for burglary in Newcastle-upon-Tyne. Others were of a warlike frame of mind, such as William who in 1312 pledged himself and his horse to the service of Edward II of England.

The chronicler Froissart records the deeds of another vicar of North Berwick, called

William, chaplain to the Earl of Douglas at the battle of Otterburn (1388):

> *The whole night he had followed the Earl with his battle-axe in hand, and had by his exertions more than once repulsed the English. This conduct gained the thanks of his countrymen. In the same year he was promoted to the archdeaconry and made Canon of Aberdeen.*

Relics of St Andrew the Apostle (an arm bone and several finger bones) had reached St Andrews, and were displayed in a purpose-made reliquary of gold and crystal (perhaps a hollow forearm and hand raised in blessing).

A ferry service was started at North Berwick, with a hospice staffed by the Cistercian nuns and a church (St Andrew's) close to the harbour, which catered for the thousands of pilgrims who crossed the Forth each year to St Andrews.

In 1373 the ferry boat was chosen as the heraldic symbol of the town and it appears in the charter when North Berwick became a Royal Burgh. A stone mould for pilgrims' badges, dating from the 14th century, has been discovered in the old parish church at the harbour.

During the late 16th century, James Melville, Professor of Hebrew at St Andrews University, wrote that the ferry boat which took him over the water, having been used for carrying coal, was 'old and dirty (and so was the ferryman)'.

Perhaps the most eminent man born in the parish was the theologian and historian John Major, born at nearby Gleghornie. He studied at the universities of Oxford, Cambridge and Paris. Major was a leading exponent of

GEORGE
BUCHANAN

scholastic philosophy and leader of those who opposed Renaissance views of Man and God. Among his students at St Andrews University were the reformers George Buchanan and Patrick Hamilton (later burned for his beliefs). Major also lectured to John Knox and was in Trinity Church, St Andrews in 1547 when Knox preached his first public sermon in which he criticised the Church and called for reform.

TRAPRAIN

Thenew or (Thanea), daughter of the sixth century chieftain King Loth, lived on Traprain Law, one of the biggest and earliest attempts at urbanisation in south-east Scotland, and one of the first where iron was used.

Thenew gave birth to an illegitimate child fathered by a shepherd-boy. She was sentenced by her father to be thrown down from the hill-top at Traprain. However, she survived and instead was banished by being set adrift in an open boat at Aberlady Bay. Happily the boat drifted to Fife where she was rescued at Culross by the monks of St Serf. Thenew's son, Mungo (or Kentigern), later helped to found what became the city of Glasgow.

After Loth died, he is said to have been buried under the 'Loth Stone' near Traprain.

In the tenth century, Olaf Godfreyson, King of Dublin, raided the mouth of the Tyne and destroyed the monastery at Tyninghame.

Shortly after World War I a hoard of Roman silver was found on the west side of Traprain Law. It had been cut into strips and rolled up for melting.

One of the articles was a silver strainer

with the words '*IESUS CHRISTUS*'. It might
have been used to purify wine for Mass. It is
possible these objects were the property of the
monastery at Tyninghame, only five miles
from Traprain.

TYNINGHAME (*destroyed in* AD 941)

In his Church History, Bede the chronicler
writes of a man of evil habits who lived at
Tyninghame.

When the man died, his soul was escorted
by an angel, first to visit Purgatory, then to the
mouth of Hell itself. The man pleaded with
the angel for another chance to live on Earth.
He was allowed to have it.

Arriving on Earth he was welcomed with
amazement by his weeping relatives. His way
of life changed completely. He became a
monk, entering a monastery, gladly accepting
all its hardships.

WHITEKIRK

In 1413 some 15,653 pilgrims were said to
have visited St Mary's, Whitekirk and its holy
well. Under the protection of James I, hostels
were built for travellers, one of whom was the
Italian diplomat **AENEAS SILVIUS PICCOLOMINI**
(1405-64), whose ship was almost wrecked in
a storm outside the mouth of the river Tyne
in the winter of 1435.

Piccolomini (later Pope Pius II) had prayed
to God to rescue him, vowing he would find
the nearest church and thank God for his
deliverance. In his bare feet he had to walk
five miles over the frozen ground – and as a
result he suffered from rheumatism for the
rest of his life!

EDINBURGH
Pre-Reformation

PRE-HISTORY

Hidden from sight in Edinburgh are the remains of ancient centres of piety and culture – standing stones, such as the Caiystane at Fairmilehead, or the silent witness of Huly Hill, engulfed by noise and traffic at the Newbridge roundabout.

Not far away, inside the perimeter of Edinburgh Airport, is the Catstane, a massive unhewn pre-historic block which was later used as the focus of 50 early long cist Christian burials, with bodies in a foetal position, laid out in nine parallel rows.

BLACKFRIARS

A Dominican (Blackfriars) priory was established south of the Cowgate around 1230. Universal preaching was their special mission. The Blackfriars would set off in pairs to teach and preach (always in English or Scots and always on foot) to communities within a 30 mile radius of the city.

In 1492 a small chapel was erected near the Dominican church by Walter Bertram, burgess of Edinburgh. Here a family requiem mass was celebrated annually with Gregorian chant accompanied by the organ and with the flicker of lighted candles on the altar.

In addition, 50 portions of bread, ale and

meat were placed on the altar and later distributed to the poor.

In 1503 the Dominicans housed the English visitors who arrived for the marriage of James IV and Princess Margaret of England.

The lower chamber of the priory was also used for meetings – annually by the Incorporation of Hammermen, and also in 1506 by the Lords of Exchequer.

THE CONVENT OF ST CATHERINE OF SIENA

A priest of St Giles, Sir John Crawford, *mortified* (bequeathed) 22 acres to sustain a chapel erected in honour of John the Baptist on the Burgh Muir. He instructed that there should be a hermit living there, clothed in white, with the image of the head of John the Baptist on his chest. The hermit was employed to clean the chapel and assist the chaplain.

On the site of the chapel in later years, the Dominican convent of St Catherine of Siena was founded by Lady Janet, widow of the 5th Lord Seton. The first prioress was Josina Henderson and the nuns became distinguished for their piety and goodness.

This was the last Roman Catholic foundation in Edinburgh before the Reformation. In 1544 the convent was attacked by the English. Twenty-three years later all its possessions passed into the hands of laymen. The only remains of the original Sciennes convent are carved keystones and bosses built into the doorways of Greyfriars Kirk.

DUDDINGSTON

The land of the parish of Duddingston was

feued by David I to Kelso Abbey and the church itself built around 1120.

The church has many interesting architectural features. The original southern entrance has a stone carving of Christ on the Cross (curiously with a long gown reaching to his feet) and another of St Peter with a drawn sword in his hand.

GREYFRIARS

The first friars of the Strict Observance (Observantines) arrived in Edinburgh from the Netherlands in 1447. Friar Cornelius, their leader, refused to live in the buildings they had been allocated near the Grassmarket until they were officially made property of the Order.

Despite public objections, the Archbishop of St Andrews gave them to the friars to be occupied by them as strangers and pilgrims according to their rule. By 1467 a Scottish Franciscan province was fully recognised.

The reputation of Friar Cornelius was such that he attracted Scots intellectuals from many parts of Europe (including the universities of Paris and Cologne), who asked to be admitted to the Order.

As well as providing food for the hungry and homeless, the Franciscans specialised in preaching, hearing confessions, and healing. The Franciscan Order was the first in Europe to place medicine on a scientific basis. In 1461 Friar Crannok was appointed physician in Edinburgh to Queen Mary of Gueldres.

HOLYROOD

Legend relates that the prolific founder of

monasteries, **DAVID I** (*circa* 1080-1153), who loved hunting, decided one day to ride to the chase, even though it was a holy day and he had been forbidden to do so by his confessor.

As he rode through the Forest of Drumsheugh, he was suddenly confronted by a magnificent stag.

The king's horse reared up in fright and, as he fell to the ground, he just had time to see a cross of light gleaming between the antlers of the stag.

To do penance David founded a new monastery in 1128 at what was from that time called Holyrood ('holy cross').

The foundation charter gave the Augustinian canons (who had been brought from Merton Priory in Surrey) the right to erect the burgh of Canongate with full trading privileges. The King made his confessor, Alwyn, its first abbot.

Holyrood was from earliest times looked upon as the most important monastery in that part of Scotland. Pope Alexander III, for example, sent a legate to Holyrood in 1180 where, with the assistance of four Scottish bishops, he excommunicated Hugh, a royal chaplain who had been made Bishop of St Andrews by King William. The Pope also excommunicated the King and placed an Interdict on Scotland.

By 1250 the Abbey of Holyrood had appropriated another 27 churches, whose revenues it received.

Holyrood's most treasured relic was the Black Rood of Scotland, a fragment of the True Cross, said to have been given by Queen Margaret to her husband, Malcolm Canmore.

David II lost it to the English in 1346 at the battle of Neville's Cross and, until the

Reformation, it was kept in Durham Cathedral. During the 'Rough Wooing' (forced marriage alliance wars) by Henry VIII in the 1540s, the font and lectern of Holyrood were forcibly removed to St Albans.

Under James V, the abbeys of Holyrood, Kelso and Melrose were given to three of his illegitimate children, who held them as *commendators* (administrators).

When riots took place in Edinburgh in 1558, and statues and religious images were damaged and ballads circulated which attacked the clergy, it was to Holyrood that preachers were summoned to account for their actions.

KING
HENRY VIII

MAGDALEN CHAPEL

The Magdalen Chapel was founded by Michael Macqueheen in 1503 on the site of the Maison Dieu, a ruined hospital. It was further endowed by Janet Rynd, his widow, who dedicated it to St Mary Magdalene and granted it in 1547 to the Incorporation of Hammermen.

ST CATHERINE'S BALM WELL

In the grounds of Liberton House stands St Catherine's Well, the 'Oily Well'. Its strange waters hide a secret healing ingredient whose powers were understood in former centuries.

Liberton may have been a leper colony in days gone by – hence the name Clapperfield (from the wooden 'clappers' used to warn off those who did not have the disease).

Legend relates that QUEEN MARGARET OF SCOTLAND (*circa* 1046-93) asked one of her ladies-in-waiting to go to Mount Sinai in Egypt and bring back some holy oil from the tomb of St Catherine of Alexandria (who in AD 307 had been tortured on the wheel – 'Catherine's Wheel' – and then beheaded by the Emperor Maximinus for publicly admitting she was a Christian).

On the lady-in-waiting's return, some of the oil was accidentally spilt on the ground as she approached Edinburgh. Soon a black, oily substance rose to the surface, later known as balsam of brimstone.

The lady-in-waiting built a chapel on the spot and was later buried there. The oil became known as Balm Oil of St Catherine and was used as a cure for arthritis, rheumatism, dislocations, inflammations, bruises, burns, sprains, and for diseases of the skin such as eczema, scabies and even leprosy.

In fact, the well (8 feet, 6 inches deep) is a bituminous spring rising through the 'parrot' coal seams below the surface. An early analysis of the water in the well found it contained soluble sulphates, chlorites and alkalis, as well as calcareous carbonates.

Nuns from the nearby convent of St Catherine of Siena used to make an annual pilgrimage to the well. James IV is recorded as having made an offering in 1504 at the chapel of St Catherine's Oily Well.

KING
JAMES VI *and* I

In 1617 James VI ordered the well to be improved with stone and steps and a door. But in 1650, when Oliver Cromwell came to Edinburgh, he dismissed the well as a 'relic of idolatry' and instructed his men to deface it and its surroundings.

ST CUTHBERT'S

Around AD 850 the Northumberland monastery of Lindisfarne had an outpost in Edinburgh – probably near the site of the present St Cuthbert's. King David I endowed the church in 1127 with a piece of land.

In the following year he gave the church and its endowments, along with its dependent chapels at Liberton and Corstorphine, to the Augustinian canons of Holyrood.

ST GILES

Edinburgh had a parish church as early as AD 854. During the reign of Alexander I (*circa* 1077-1124) the church was dedicated to the environmentally-friendly St Giles who was usually depicted standing beside a deer, an arrow through his hand.

The SEAL *of* ST GILES

Giles was said to have been born in Athens around AD 640. He gave all his goods to the poor and sailed to France where, in dense forestland, he lived the life of a hermit, existing on roots, herbs and the milk of a deer hind.

In later centuries, St Giles became the patron of woodlands, lepers, beggars, cripples and those affected by disaster or otherwise marginalised by society.

It was William Preston of Gorton, near Liberton, who, with the help of the French nobility, brought an arm bone of St Giles to Edinburgh. He bequeathed it to St Giles Kirk where the Preston Aisle was constructed in 1454 soon after his death.

Every 1st September since the twelfth century, a solemn procession was made through the streets of Edinburgh, to celebrate the feast of St Giles.

A life-size wooden statue of the saint, brightly-painted and decorated with coloured drapes, formed the focal point of this event. During the procession the reliquary of St Giles was also displayed.

Parish churches were the poorest part of the ecclesiastical system in the Middle Ages and the citizens of Edinburgh complained in 1419 that the Kirk of St Giles had long before been surreptitiously given to the Augustinians at Scone.

A 1466 charter of James III and the agreement of the Pope in 1468 made St Giles Kirk a collegiate church with a provost, a dean, 16 prebendaries (canons), a choirmaster, four choristers, a sacristan, beadle and enough chaplains to celebrate Mass at the 36 altars in the church. The primary function of these 'colleagues' was to offer masses in perpetuity for the dead founder, his friends and heirs. As a collegiate church, St Giles ranked with the greatest on the Continent.

The poet GAVIN DOUGLAS (1474-1522), son of the 5th Earl of Angus, became provost of St Giles in 1503 and lived in his official residence on the site of the present Parliament House and Advocates' Library. In 1515 he became Bishop of Dunkeld and moved to the Cowgate opposite Blackfriars' Wynd. It was here on 15th May 1556 that John Knox preached to the biggest audience he had ever had in Edinburgh, continuing over a period of ten days.

The chapel of St Elois in St Giles became the property of the Incorporation of Hammermen in 1496. In the chapel hung the Blue Blanket, said to have been carried by Scottish craftsmen during the Crusades. In fact the banner was presented to the city in 1482 by James II, giving citizens the right of calling out the trained bands to fight under it when the town was in danger.

ST MARGARET'S CHAPEL

Constructed in the eleventh century, the chapel is the oldest surviving building in Edinburgh. Built on the highest part of the Castle Rock, its simple lines, with walls of whitewashed stone and glowing stained-glass, are reminders of the civilising piety of Queen Margaret of Scotland, after whom the chapel is named. Her Christian charity was evident to all in the kingdom – she maintained 24 needy persons, fed 300 poor in the great hall, gave help to orphans, and established standards for the practice of religion, acceding to the decline of the native Celtic monasticism by inviting members of the international monastic Orders to Scotland.

ST MARGARET'S CHAPEL, EDINBURGH CASTLE

ST TRIDUANA'S, RESTALRIG

Born at Colossae, Turkey in the 4th century, Triduana (Tredwell) was said to have accompanied St Regulus (Rule) on his flight from Greece to Scotland with St Andrew's relics.

For a number of years Triduana led an enclosed life as a nun at Rescobie in Forfar. She was of aristocratic birth, a beautiful and highly virtuous woman.

Although a local nobleman, Prince Nectan, wanted to marry Triduana, she had no intention of accepting. She asked the Prince's messengers what it was that so appealed to him and discovered that it was the beauty of her eyes. Triduana told the messengers, 'What he admires in me, he shall have'.

She left the room, gouged out her eyes and came back with them impaled on a wooden skewer. 'Take what your Prince so much desires,' she said to the messengers of Nectan.

After this extraordinary self-mutilation to preserve her life as a nun, Triduana crossed the Forth and settled at Restalrig, near Edinburgh, devoting herself to prayer and fasting until her death many years later.

Even while she was alive, Restalrig became a place of pilgrimage for those who suffered from diseases of the eye.

In 1477 James III endowed a chaplaincy in the upper chapel of the parish church of the Holy Trinity and Blessed Virgin of Restalrig – this later became a Chapel Royal.

Ten years afterwards, Pope Innocent VIII upgraded the chapel into a collegiate church. By 1496, when James IV had succeeded his father (who died at the battle of Sauchieburn), there were eight *prebendaries* (canons) under a dean. One canon was in charge of the music, another was sacristan. Each had a room and a garden and there was a singing school for choirboys. When James IV was killed at Flodden in 1513, the requiem masses for the dead sung at Restalrig must have been doubly poignant, for he had been an enthusiastic patron of the shrine. Within two years James V completed the foundation at Restalrig, the parish church of Leith, himself placing the final coping-stone.

TRINITY COLLEGE

The College was established in 1460 by **QUEEN MARY OF GUELDRES** (*d* 1463), widow of James II, to provide divine worship and for the care of 14 poor *bedesmen* (pensioners), with a provost and ten priests or clerks.

Whenever one of the priests said mass, he had to process in his vestments, carrying a hyssop plant, to the tomb of the foundress and recite the *De Profundis* ('Out of the depths').

During the early sixteenth century, rich covers were used on the altar. There were curtains with silk fringes around the head of the statue of the Virgin Mary. Silver chalices and reliquaries were employed and services were enlivened by organs and bells. The magnificent Trinity College altarpiece is still preserved in the National Gallery of Scotland.

The Dean of Trinity College had to be a Doctor of Laws and, after the establishment of the Court of Session in 1532, was usually its President.

The HAND-WRITING *of* MARY *of* GUELDRES

MIDLOTHIAN
Pre-Reformation

PRE-HISTORY

Although there are no Neolithic burial monuments in Midlothian, the Ordnance Survey triangulation pillar on the summit of Soutra Hill stands on a flat-topped barrow. At Crichton Mains a souterrain can be seen, whose walls incorporate numerous blocks of Roman ashlar. At Auchencorth stands the two-metre high Gowk Stone.

In the village of Borthwick there are fragments of three early Christian burials, including cross-shafts with relief carving of fantastic beasts. More than fifty cists, aligned east to west and containing inhumations, fill the cemetery at Newfarm.

NEWBATTLE

The earliest parts of the Abbey date from the twelfth century when Ralph, a Cistercian monk sent from Melrose to build up the new community, became its first abbot. He was 'a young man of great saintliness – a person of beautiful presence, continually occupied in divine meditation who, from his youth, loved his Creator with all his heart'. Indeed such was his piety that he was apparently of special interest to Satan – Abbot Ralph is said to have seen the Devil in the woods at Newbattle, with 'a face as black as pitch'.

The monastery had large estates in the Lothians, in Lanark, Peebles and Stirling and at one time had a community of 80 monks and 70 lay-brothers.

Some of the monks mined coal. Lay-brothers extracted salt from sea-water; others constructed carts; many were involved in forestry, sheep farming or horse-breeding. The famous Clydesdale workhorse was developed at Newbattle, and the Musselburgh leek and other vegetables were introduced into Scotland by the Newbattle monks.

There were many craftsmen associated with the Abbey – silversmiths and goldsmiths, candlemakers, blacksmiths, weavers and corn-millers all worked on the estates. The monks also ran the Customs service on the east coast of Lothian.

The achievements of the monks made the Abbey a prime target for marauding English armies. In 1296 King Edward I came to Newbattle, and in 1385, under Richard II, the English burned the Abbey and several of its farms.

Defensive peel towers built by the monks were destroyed. Some monks were taken away as prisoners, some fled to other monasteries. The few left were forced to sell 29 chalices, nine crosses, other ornaments and all their silver plate to buy food. Most of the Abbey tower was ruined in the fire when the stone cross fell down through the roof.

One of the high points of the monastery's political life came in 1503: Margaret Tudor was entertained at the Abbey before her marriage to James IV (who visited her daily at Newbattle).

Over the next few years the Abbey was rebuilt, but in 1544 the English Earl of

Hertford and his army invaded Scotland. As one chronicle put it, 'upon the 15th day of May, the horsemen raid to Newbottill and brynt it'.

Retribution came when **MARY OF LORRAINE (MARY OF GUISE**, 1515-60) held a convention of the Lords of her party at Newbattle in 1547, prior to declaring war against England.

NEWTON

Margaret, daughter of Sir John Herries of Newton, was very religious and beautiful. She often visited Newbattle Abbey and there in 1375 she fell in love with a young Cistercian monk whom she subsequently met secretly at a little farm nearby. The owner of the farm was a widow and she also had a lover who was a Newbattle monk.

Sir John discovered the relationship and threatened to kill his daughter if she did not end the affair. She agreed to stop seeing the monk.

One night Sir John went into Margaret's room and found the bed empty. He set off for the farm, attempted to get into the farmhouse and, being unable to do so, set fire to the thatch in the roof. In the conflagration which followed, nine people died, including his daughter, the widow and the two monks.

Sir John was eventually pardoned on condition that he 'should, bareheaded and barelegged, in sackcloth, crave absolution at the bishop's and abbot's hands, and stand in the same manner at the principal door of St Catherine's chapel every Sabbath and holy day for one year, paying forty pennies at every time to the poor of the parish, and one hundred merks to the monks of Newbattle to pray for the souls of those who died through his transgression'. The tragic story is recorded in Sir Walter Scott's 'Gray Brother'.

Over the last centuries a 'grey lady' has been seen from time to time in what remains of the old monastic cellar under the present house. Then in 1990, while building work was taking place, human remains were discovered – the bodies of monks who had been buried in the precincts of the Abbey. Two of them may have been those of the monks who died in the farm cottage fire.

In a moving ecumenical service the remains were later reinterred in the presence of the Abbot of the Cistercian Abbey of Nunraw. From that time the ghostly figure of the 'grey lady' ceased to be seen.

ROSLIN

The Collegiate Church of St Matthew, founded in 1446 by Prince William Sinclair (the last of his family to be Prince of Orkney) is only half-completed.

Below ground-level the vaults contain the bodies of twelve Sinclair knights, buried in full armour between 1484 and 1650, among them Sir William de Sincler, Grand Prior of the Knights Templar. Preserved in 'The Lay of the Last Minstrel', a poem by Sir Walter Scott (who had a house close by), is the legend that when a member of the Sinclair family dies, the chapel glows red.

Perhaps the most celebrated member of the Sinclair family was **PRINCE HENRY SINCLAIR** (1345- *circa* 1400), born in nearby Rosslyn Castle. Supported financially by the

Knights Templar, he organised an expedition of twelve ships for a voyage to the New World, where he landed at the future Nova Scotia in 1398, a century before Christopher Columbus.

Settling among the indians, he taught them how to fish with nets and how to raise crops. After many adventures he returned to Orkney, where he was murdered around the year 1400 and buried in St Matthew's.

Henry's grandson, William, commemorated the voyage to America by ordering carvings of some of the exotic plants Henry had brought back across the Atlantic to be placed in the chapel – such as the aloa cactus and sweetcorn.

There are 56 different masons' marks on the walls of the chapel, reminding the curious of Hiram Abiff, the architect of Solomon's temple, who is credited as being the first to carve a mason's mark.

Although used as a stable by Cromwell's troops in 1650, the chapel was undamaged. Cromwell was himself a Grand Master Mason and knew the importance of the building to Freemasonry.

In the chapel two pillars stand together, a plain one and a highly ornamented one – the Master Mason's Pillar and the Prentice Pillar (in which the Holy Grail is rumoured to be hidden).

The story goes that, before beginning to carve his pillar, the master mason decided to go abroad to increase his knowledge of the art of stone-carving.

In his absence, his apprentice had a dream that he had carved his master's pillar and, on waking, the apprentice begged William Sinclair to be allowed to carve it.

He was given permission and carved an

The PRENTICE PILLAR, ROSLIN CHAPEL

elaborate and original representation of the Tree of Life, showing eight winged dragons having eaten the grapes of wrath, with a vine-tree emerging from their mouths, sucking the poison out to allow the tree to grow pure and strong.

The master mason returned. He saw the masterpiece his apprentice had carved and was racked with rage and jealousy. In his fury he struck the apprentice on the head, killing him instantly.

Inside the chapel can be seen the contents of King Solomon's herb garden, carved in stone; while among the flying buttresses on the outside of the chapel are sunflowers and howling gargoyles, emphasising the half-pagan exoticism of the shrine.

SOUTRA

Between the A7 and the A68, on the 1200 feet slope of Soutra Hill high on the Fala Moors south of Edinburgh, the remains of Soutra Hospital are being excavated.

The name 'Soutra' comes from the Brythonic *Sol Tref* (outlook house). The Church and Hospital of the Holy Trinity, halfway between Melrose and Holyrood, was founded in 1164 by Malcolm IV and administered by Augustinian canons.

It was staffed by a Master, eight prebendaries, two clerks or choristers, with up to 13 poor people in the Hospital. It had the privilege of sanctuary which was marked off by a chain suspended on Cross Chainhill. Trinity Well on the north of the hill provided mineral water to refresh and restore good health.

Between 1453-55 the Hospital fell into ruin and was not used for hospitality. In 1462 it was annexed to Trinity College in Edinburgh and restored to the status of a Hospital and parish church under a vicar appointed by the provost of Trinity. By then only three poor people were living at Soutra.

Soutra, nevertheless, continued to operate on a reduced basis until around 1630.

Soutra Hospital's mission was the care of the sick, the infirm, the aged, the poor, and travellers on the main highway which ran beside it. Later it cared for monastic pensioners (*bedesmen*).

Because of its location on the main route in and out of Edinburgh, Soutra, as a neutral religious foundation, also tended to the injuries of those wounded in battle, either Scots or English, at the time of the many incursions from south of the Border.

Blood-letting was one therapy widely used – both for those in the Hospital's care and by the Augustinian monks themselves who were bled between seven and twelve times a year as a way of cleansing the body and the mind. Medieval medicine claimed that blood-letting had many benefits, including the clearing of the brain, the strengthening of the memory, the sharpening of hearing and the cleansing of the guts!

Archaeologists have uncovered 30 blood dumps with something like 500 gallons soaked into the ground. Here they have also found spores of anthrax and tetanus, showing that plague-victims were treated at Soutra. In addition, traces of the medicines used have been discovered, including black henbane, hemlock and opium poppy, along with a 600-year old scalpel. Current investigations include a search for the AIDS virus.

TEMPLE
(*also known as* BALANTRODACH)

Temple was the Scottish headquarters of the Order of Knights Templar since 1153 when it was gifted to them by David I. The Templars were a military organisation of fighting monks who had amassed knowledge of navigation, medicine and sciences – an amalgam of Old Testament, Judaic, Islamic and Dualist thought.

Their influence was considerable – ROBERT THE BRUCE (1274-1329) is known to have been trained in martial arts at Dalhousie, only three miles from Balantrodach, and it is thought that a core of Knights Templar stiffened the victorious Scottish army led by Bruce at Bannockburn (1314).

But the Order was also controversial. In 1309 some Scots Templar knights stood trial at Holyrood before Archbishop Lamberton of St Andrews, on charges of heresy. However, they were given verdicts of not proven.

Nevertheless, Pope Clement V suppressed the international Order in 1312, although it was not officially suppressed in Scotland because Robert the Bruce had already been excommunicated for killing John Comyn in 1306. The Temple preceptory (so-called after the Christian precepts which knights promised to obey) was then given to the Knights Hospitaller of St John for safe-keeping.

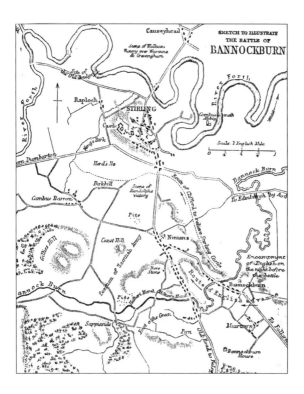

WEST LOTHIAN
Pre-Reformation

CAIRNPAPPLE

Cairnpapple (*Kernepapple* – meaning a cairn of loose stones) is known as Scotland's Stonehenge. A hill three miles north of Bathgate near Torphichen, it preserves at least five phases of ritual and burial activity and is one of the most important prehistoric monuments in Scotland, having been used as a burial and ritual site from *circa* 3000 to 1400 BC.

Today visitors can go down into a chamber containing a Beaker burial of the Early Bronze Age. An arc of holes surrounds the central chamber. In and close to the holes a number of deposits of cremated human bones were found.

A few centuries later the site was turned into a *henge* (open air temple). Twenty-four large stones were set up in an oval, surrounded by a ditch and bank, and a ceremonial burial made at the foot of the standing stone. Later, its ceremonial use was forgotten, but the hill was still used for burials. The stones of the old shrine were taken down and re-used to form the edge of a circular cairn.

In the Bronze Age the cairn was enlarged. More burials were made in the Iron Age, providing continuity of use for over 1000 years.

LINLITHGOW

Linlithgow Palace was always right in the mainstream of Scottish public life. All the Stewart kings lived here. **MARY QUEEN OF SCOTS** (1542-87) was born there.

A similar importance attaches to the 13th century St Michael's Church, in spite of the indignity the building suffered in 1302 when Edward I used it for storing wheat, wine, malt, beans, oats, salt and sea coal.

James IV habitually gave the *Skire Siller* ('Skire' means Purification Thursday – the day before Good Friday) on the steps of St Michael's. Coins used for the ceremony were specially minted at the Royal Mint, Linlithgow. Later he imitated the Last Supper, using basins of hot water filled with herbs to wash the feet of the poor. He gave them each a new gown of Dutch cloth, a pair of shoes, wooden bowls and platters.

MARY
QUEEN *of* SCOTS

The church has a special place in Scottish history, for in 1513 James IV heard his last mass there on the eve of his departure to the ill-fated battle of Flodden.

The King was kneeling in prayer at St Catherine's Aisle, when he was warned of bad luck by 'ane figure of ane blue man' if he fought against his English in-laws. The King paid no heed and died tragically at Flodden.

During the reign of James V, the vicar was **GEORGE CRICHTON**, who later became a bishop. Crichton liked to boast that he had read neither the Old nor the New Testament!

In 1542 Mary Queen of Scots was baptised in the church and **NINIAN WINZET** (*c* 1518-92), later Abbot of Ratisbon, Germany was made rector of Linlithgow grammar school.

LIVINGSTON

On New Year's morning, at the royal hunting-lodge at Newyearfield, the kings of Scotland touched people suffering from the skin disease *scrofula*. During the ceremony a sacred spring was also visited. After dipping his finger in the water, the King would place his healing hands on the sufferer.

TORPHICHEN

The Preceptory of Torphichen was the Scottish headquarters of the Knights Hospitaller of the Order of St John of Jerusalem, who first came to Scotland during the reign of David I.

In 1099 the Order, in addition to ministering to the sick and poor, adopted a role of military protection for pilgrims to the Holy Land. The Knights wore a black habit embroidered with a golden eight-pointed cross. In battle they wore a red surcoat with a plain white cross.

The Preceptory was one of the few fortified ecclesiastical buildings in Scotland, but also contained the Knights' herb garden to help them fulfil their vocation of 'helping their lords the Sick'.

The Knights staffed one of the earliest hospitals in Scotland (Magdalene's Lazar House for the treatment of lepers) and with their 'sanctuary stones' provided safety to those in trouble with the law.

It has been suggested that the sanctuary stone in the graveyard of Torphichen Kirk may have once been a sacrificial stone from Cairnpapple.

It is a small rectangular stone with a hollow (for blood?) shaped like a Maltese

Cross on top. On its east side are several cup-markings. The Knights also used the stone to mark the centre of their lands. The bounds of sanctuary extended a mile east, north, west and south, each marked with a carved stone.

In March 1530 James Inglis, Abbot of Culross, was killed by the Laird of Tulliallan and his servants. Some of the attackers claimed the right of sanctuary at the boundary stone. After trial, they were acquitted and returned to the care of the Master of Torphichen.

Before going into battle, WILLIAM WALLACE (*circa* 1274-1305) held the last of his Scottish Parliaments (the Convention of Barons) at the Preceptory on 29th March 1298. Three months later Torphichen treated Edward I after the battle of Falkirk. He had broken two ribs the night before when his horse trod on him.

Due east from the Preceptory was St John's Well, a spring of pure water, where the knights were said to go every morning for a refreshing drink.

After the Knights Templar were dissolved in the fourteenth century, many of their properties were taken over by the Knights Hospitaller.

In 1953 an octocentenary service was held at Torphichen by the Knights of St John.

WILLIAM
WALLACE

TWO

EAST LOTHIAN
Post-Reformation

ATHELSTANEFORD

One of the most interesting ministers of the kirk was **REVD ROBERT BLAIR** (1699-1746), minister from 1731-46, who is buried in the churchyard. Fascinated by poetry and botany, he wrote 'The Grave', a spine-chilling 800-line meditation on death. In 1808 twelve powerful illustrations by the poet-artist William Blake were printed for the poem:

The sickly taper,
By glimmering through the low-browed musty
   vaults
(Furred round with mouldy damps, and ropy slime)
Lets fall a supernumerary horror ...

The wind is up: hark! how it howls! methinks
Till now I never heard a sound so dreary.
Doors creak, and windows clap, and night's foul
   bird
Rooked in the spire, screams loud.

GIFFORD

Dedicated to the only clergyman to sign the American Declaration of Independence, a plaque on the garden wall of Gifford manse commemorates **JOHN WITHERSPOON** (1723-94), born in the manse and destined to be the first Moderator of the Presbyterian Church of America.

NORTH BERWICK

In 1590 around 200 witches were called to meet the Devil in North Berwick kirk. They travelled from Leith down the Forth, sailing in sieves, and crawled up the beach to the kirk of St Andrew. There they plotted to sink James VI as he sailed from Denmark to Scotland. The Devil, disguised in a horned mask, is thought to have been **FRANCIS STUART** (*circa* 1563-1612), the 5th Earl of Bothwell.

A schoolmaster from Prestonpans, John Cunningham (known as Dr Fian), blew up the doors of the kirk and blew out its lights.

The Devil stood in the pulpit, ordered the witches to open graves and make powder from the finger-joints of the dead and the witches kissed the Devil's behind before taking part in an orgy of malevolence.

Afterwards, during a show-trial, the so-called 'witches' from East Lothian and Edinburgh were tortured to confess the details of the supposed plot, which appealed to the King's obsession with witchcraft and the occult.

The poet **ROBERT BURNS** (1759-96), whose mother, brother and sister are buried at Bolton, used the story for part of his poem 'Tam o' Shanter'.

JOHN BLACKADDER (1615-86), minister of Troqueer, near Dumfries, was deprived of his parish in 1662 for his Covenanting views. Arrested in Edinburgh on 5th April 1681 for 'preaching in the fields', he was imprisoned on the Bass Rock, died there and was buried in the new parish church at North Berwick. This replaced the pre-Reformation church which had partly subsided into the sea.

PRESTONPANS

Prestonpans kirk, dating from 1596, is the earliest post-Reformation church in Lothian.

ALEXANDER 'JUPITER' CARLYLE (1722-1805), son of a Prestonpans minister, describes how he climbed the church tower in 1745 to watch the battle of Prestonpans.

After the defeat of General Cope's forces, a team of doctors and apprentice surgeons came from Edinburgh to tend the wounded. One was GEORGE HAY (1729-1811), Episcopalian and Jacobite, who later became Roman Catholic bishop for the Lowland District.

One poignant story of the battle concerned COL JAMES GARDINER of the Dragoons (1688-1745), originally a West Lothian man. On a July night in 1719, reading Thomas Watson's poem 'Christian Soldier', he fell asleep and dreamt of a blaze of light illuminating the book and Christ hanging on the cross surrounded with glory. A voice spoke: 'O sinner, did I suffer this for thee and are these the returns?' Gardiner awoke and was converted.

On 21st September 1745 near his home, Bankton House, Gardiner was pulled from his horse and savagely attacked by a Highlander wielding a Lochaber axe. The Colonel dragged himself over the battlefield and, Christ-like, fell under a local landmark, the Thorn Tree. He was shot eight times, with six cuts to his head. He died at a nearby Tranent manse that evening in the arms of the minister's niece, and was buried in the kirk-yard at Tranent.

THE HADDINGTON PILGRIMAGE

Since 1971 the ecumenical Haddington Pilgrimage has taken place each Spring. The

Pilgrimage opens with a service in nearby Whitekirk Parish Church, after which pilgrims walk, bicycle or drive to St Mary's, Haddington where services continue throughout the day; as well as at the tiny chapel at Lennoxlove, not far from Haddington.

At Whitekirk the Revd **TOM CUTHELL**, minister of St Cuthbert's in Edinburgh and one of the organising committee, commented:

> *There are a number of good reasons why people come on the Pilgrimage. I think it's a tremendous boost to one's spiritual morale to be part of a great company travelling together on the same road. Also I like to think there is a momentum here for closer unity between Christians. We still cannot worship at the same altar, at the same holy table, but, God willing, that will come in the future. Haddington also highlights the divisions between the churches and we pray for the healing of the wounds that still lacerate the body of Christ.*

Although St Mary's is a Church of Scotland kirk, the tiny Episcopal Chapel of the Three Kings forms part of the Lauderdale family burial vaults. Patrick Maitland, the present Earl of Lauderdale, was for many years the driving-force behind the Pilgrimage:

> *I'm over eighty now. I've had a very exciting life. I've travelled the world as a newspaperman. I once escaped being murdered in Albania by hiding in a harem. I've also had the privilege of being in Parliament. In the evening of my life the discovery of this pilgrimage and the event of bringing people together for healing and unity of love is the greatest thing in my life – all in the name of Christ Our Lord and his Mother.*

EDINBURGH
Post-Reformation

BRISTO MEETING-HOUSE

In March 1738 a grand convention for followers of the Seceding ministers was held in a square plain on the Braid Hills for a congregation of 5000.

Four years later the Bristo Meeting-House opened and was soon the stronghold of the Secession movement. During the Jacobite capture of Edinburgh, the Seceders worshipped in open-air services at Dreghorn near the Pentland Hills.

ADAM GIB, the first minister, was known as 'Pope Gib'. In his service he attacked the English evangelist George Whitefield.

This was the oldest of the Secession congregations. In 1747 the 'Breach' between *Burghers* and *Anti-burgers* took place there. It was also there that they united again in 1820 – the first Synod of the United Presbyterian Church taking place in 1847 .

THOMAS CARLYLE (1795-1881) heard Glen, a Burgher minister, preach at Bristo:

> *I heard Glen preach for the last time in Peddie's Meeting-House, a large, fine place behind Bristo Street – night just sinking as he ended and the tone of his voice betokening how full the heart was.*

CANONGATE KIRK

James VII wrote to the Privy Council in June 1687 of his intention to restore the ancient Order of the Thistle and make the church of Holyroodhouse the Chapel of the Order, to be conducted according to the Roman Catholic rite. Parishioners of Canongate, who had worshipped at the Abbey church there since 1561, were to be ejected. The lofts, galleries, seats and pews of the church were to be removed and reused in Canongate Kirk to be built in 1691 further up the Royal Mile. This explains why the monarch is both a parishioner of the Canongate Kirk and a seat-holder.

Edinburgh Castle was once in the parish of Holyrood Abbey. After the Reformation it was joined to the Canongate Kirk. In the kirkyard are buried soldiers who have died at the Castle.

THE CONVENT OF
ST CATHERINE OF SIENA

At the Reformation, the convent's buildings – kirk, yards and houses – were demolished. The nuns were expelled and sold the land to make some money to live on. They survived in poverty with their friends and families.

LORD HENRY COCKBURN (1779-1854) wrote in *Memorials of His Time* that 'a part of the monastery of the nuns of Sienna (from which the neighbouring village, now part of Edinburgh, is called Sciennes or 'Sheens') stood in a field behind our house and a fragment of the monastery still remains'.

This relic of the old monastery stood until 1871, when it was removed to build a semi-detached villa. A plaque was at that time placed on the wall to mark the site of the monastery. The last fragments of the convent were removed around 1910 to make way for yet another new villa in St Catherine's Place.

DUDDINGSTON

Shortly after the Reformation, **JOHN BRAND**, previously an Augustinian canon at Holyrood, was appointed Reader at Duddingston. He was a preacher of great power and served in the church until 1588.

ROBERT MENTEATH (*circa* 1621-60) was the son of an Edinburgh burgess who had the lease of a salmon fishing in the Forth. Menteath taught philosophy at the University of Saumur in France.

He returned to Edinburgh and became minister of Duddingston, but had to flee back to France in disgrace. There he became a Roman Catholic and was made secretary to Cardinal Richelieu.

One day the Cardinal asked him from which branch of the Menteaths he was descended. He said 'from the Menteaths of *salmon-net!*' Later he was appointed a canon at Notre Dame Cathedral.

REVD JOHN THOMSON (1778-1840), sometimes known as the 'Father of Scottish Landscapists', formed a village choir which he accompanied on the violin. One member was John Wilson, the tenor. Thomson also played the flute.

Thomson referred to his congregation as 'ma bairns' and they in turn responded 'we're a' *Jock Tamson's bairns'* – today a Scottish by-word for universal fellowship.

Down at the bottom of his garden, by the edge of Duddingston Loch, Thomson had a

studio from 1810-1840 in the upper floor of
an octagonal tower he called 'Edinburgh'.
When he wanted to be alone Thomson
retreated to the tower, instructing his house-
keeper to inform visitors that the minister
was 'in Edinburgh'!

Sir Walter
Scott

Sir Walter Scott (1771-1832)
was an elder at Duddingston and
is said to have written part of *The
Heart of Midlothian* in the manse
garden. Another elder was Louis
Cauvin (1754-1825), founder of
the Dean orphanage, who in 1787,
at his premises in the High Street,
taught French to the poet Robert
Burns.

THE FRIARIES

Shortly before the Reformation, when parish
clergy had become increasingly decadent in
morals and religion, it was the friars (the
Dominicans and Franciscans) who continued
to observe faithfully the traditional vows of
poverty, chastity and obedience.

Within the precincts of the Dominican
priory in Edinburgh a final Provincial Council
was held in 1549 to make reforms against
concubinage in the hierarchy, the ignorance
of literature and the liberal arts among the
parish clergy, and the 'profane obscenity of
life' among churchmen of all ranks, as well as
the misappropriation of the funds of hospitals
and endowments for the poor.

A further council met in Edinburgh in
1552, preoccupied by the fact that 'very few
out of the most populous parishes deign to be
present at the sacrifice of holy Mass on Sundays
and festivals'. A new catechism was approved

and the parish clergy were instructed to read from it to their people every Sunday.

In the months of March and April 1559 a final council met to consider proposals for the correction of abuses in the life of the clergy. This was the last official act of the Roman Catholic Church as Scotland's established church.

But the proposed reforms came too late and also encouraged many young churchmen to embrace the Protestant Reformation.

John Knox arrived in Leith on 2nd May. In spite of the Provost of Edinburgh and other sympathisers sleeping alternate nights in the two friaries, the people of the burgh broke down the gates and entered both buildings, removing everything that they could carry, leaving nothing but bare walls without doors or windows. At the beginning of July the Dominican and Franciscan friaries in Edinburgh were destroyed.

Nevertheless, a Convention of the Reformed Kirk, meeting in Leith in 1572, decided that archbishoprics and bishoprics should remain and that cathedral chapters should not be disturbed until the last member died. Indeed abbots and priors were constitutionally necessary – as Members of Parliament and as Senators in the College of Justice.

THE GLASITE MEETING-HOUSE

The Church of Christ (Glasite) was founded by **REVD JOHN GLAS** (1695-1773). He was a minister who was forced to leave his charge at Tealing, Angus in 1728 because he chose to preach the Gospel of Christ, rather than denounce Episcopacy or Roman Catholicism, as he was then required to do.

By the time of his death, Glas had set up some 30 churches worldwide. Edinburgh's Glasite Meeting-house in Barony Street was commissioned in 1834 and reflects the simplicity of the Glasite service of Bible readings, prayers and unaccompanied psalms which lasted for most of the day. Services began in the large top-lit main hall with its box pews holding 200 persons. Lunch was taken in the elegant first floor Feast Room, the faithful sharing their single-pot kail meals.

GREYFRIARS KIRK

Greyfriars was the first church to be constructed in Edinburgh after the Reformation. The new church was built in the garden of the former Franciscan monastery. Buttresses, doors and stone shields and bosses from the convent of St Catherine at Sciennes were used in its construction.

The church was opened in December 1620 with a pulpit taken from the High School, a Bible and a green cloth. There were no pews, only stools which the congregation themselves supplied. During the sermon the men kept their hats on.

Greyfriars has a central part in the history of the National Covenant, a protest by Scottish Presbyterians against new English forms of worship introduced by Charles I.

The first copy of the document was drawn up in the Tailors' Hall, Cowgate and then brought up to Greyfriars on 27th February 1638, to be signed by nobles and lairds and by ministers and representatives of the Scottish towns.

When, in June 1679, the Covenanters were finally defeated at Bothwell Bridge, 1200 of

SIGNING *the* NATIONAL COVENANT

them were roped in pairs and imprisoned
outside Greyfriars Kirk, living in the open
for five months with no shelter and little
food.

Four hundred Covenanters were sentenced
to be transported to the West Indies, but
many were released after promising not to
rebel again. Others 'gave glory to God' in the
Grassmarket before their execution.

The West Lothian Covenanter, **ALEXANDER
REID**, records in his autobiography the dying
words of a 26-year old man called McKail, who
had previously come from Edinburgh to assist

in GREYFRIARS KIRKYARD *on* 27TH FEBRUARY 1638

the Covenanters at nearby Pentland. McKail was arrested, imprisoned in Edinburgh and tortured with 'the boots'. His legs were placed in iron casings and wedges driven in to compress and eventually crush his legs.

Memorably, McKail prayed:

Farewell sun, moon and stars.
Farewell, kindred and friends.
Farewell, world and time.
Farewell, weak and frail body.
Welcome eternity.
Welcome angels and saints.

*Welcome, Saviour of the world
and welcome God, the judge of all.*

Five men were hanged in chains and 250 sent by sea to the West Indies. Off Orkney the ship sank in a storm. Most of the Covenanters were drowned. In a long trench in the kirkyard 100 other Covenanters lie buried.

When Episcopalian worship was introduced into Edinburgh, **ANDREW RAMSAY** (1574-1659), minister of Greyfriars, refused to read the Service book. So Ramsay was relieved of his charge by the bishops. He became a leading Covenanter in the north of Scotland, but returned to preach in Greyfriars shortly before the signing of the National Covenant.

ROBERT TRAIL (1603-76), minister of Greyfriars, was imprisoned in Edinburgh Castle and later denounced as a Pentland rebel (Covenanter). He was imprisoned on the Bass Rock in the Firth of Forth. Perhaps the most frightening moment of his career had come on a Sunday morning in 1659 when a storm nearly took the roof off Greyfriars church. Trail and his congregation, however, escaped.

By 1561 Greyfriars had been turned into two churches with a dividing wall to accommodate an increase in the city parishes.

Sir Walter Scott attended Greyfriars with his parents. The church appears in his novel *Guy Mannering*. Leaving the church one morning, Scott fell in love with Williamina Belches with whom he shared his umbrella.

On 19th January 1845 fire burned everything in the church except the walls. But Greyfriars was reopened in 1857 with **DR JOHN LEE** (1779-1859) as minister. He introduced innovations in worship which caused a furore in the Church of Scotland – standing during praise, kneeling at prayer, the use of instrumental music, the celebration of marriages in church, stained-glass windows and other church ornaments. Greyfriars was the first Presbyterian church in Scotland to introduce these.

THE HEBREW COMMUNITY

Although there had been individual Jews resident in Edinburgh from at least 1750, it was not until 1816 that the first regular Synagogue was established and 1820 before the Jewish community publicly announced their celebration of the Feast of Tabernacles in a building in a lane off Nicolson Street – the first Hebrew Congregation in Scotland.

The first Jews in Edinburgh came from Russian Poland, Germany and the Baltic ports. Although a piece of ground had been purchased near the Calton Jail in 1819, it was at Braid Place that the first Jewish cemetery proper was established in 1820. Later a cemetery was opened at Echobank.

HOLYROOD ABBEY

Holyrood frequently played a provocative role in the religious life of Edinburgh.

On a drizzly day in August 1561, Mary Queen of Scots arrived to live in Holyrood, which remained her home in Edinburgh.

The first minister there was former Dominican friar JOHN CRAIG (1512-1600). He proclaimed the banns between Mary Queen of Scots and Lord Henry Darnley, but later refused to publish those between Mary and Lord James Bothwell.

When Charles I brought Archbishop

William Laud to Edinburgh in 1633, the Abbey Church was prepared for his coronation with an altar and candles. Equally offensive to Presbyterian Edinburgh was the consecration at the Abbey on 6th May 1662 of four bishops.

Late in 1686 James VII's yacht arrived from London with an altar, vestments, statues and priests for a new Roman Catholic Chapel Royal to be set up at Holyrood. Not many months later the outraged parishioners of Holyrood were evicted.

LADY YESTER'S CHURCH, INFIRMARY STREET

The minor functionaries of Edinburgh churches sometimes created for themselves a sub-culture of comic subterfuge. In 'Portraits', the razor-eyed barber and caricaturist, JOHN KAY (1742-1826), supplies a vivid word-picture of the beadle at Lady Yester's Church in Infirmary Street – Mungo Watson.

> *Mungo was a living chronicle of the Presbyterian Church, or rather of the passing events in what he called the religious world. He was keeper of the hall for the meetings of the Society for the Propagation of Christian Knowledge, beadle of Lady Yester's Church, and one of the door-keepers during the General Assembly.*
>
> *During the sittings of the General Assembly, he contrived, in his capacity of door-keeper, to make the most of the situation, and pocketed as much of 'the needful' as he could possibly extract by an embargo upon visitors. He was highly esteemed by a large circle of old ladies of the middle ranks, who eagerly listened to the gossip he contrived to pick up in the course of the day.*

MAGDALEN CHAPEL

The stained-glass windows of the chapel faced
a nobleman's garden and so escaped destruction
during the Reformation and are the only
pre-Reformation stained-glass windows in
Scotland still in situ.

The chapel was the meeting-place of the
first General Assembly of the Church of
Scotland (20th December 1560) with 42
members (only six being ministers, including
John Knox, no moderator having been chosen).

There the Assembly ordered that the kirk
of Restalrig be 'razed and utterly cast down
and destroyed' because it was a 'monument of
idolatry'. It sanctioned the appointment of

35 ministers and eight readers and petitioned Parliament that only those accepting the Reformed religion should hold office.

Another Assembly took place in the Chapel in April 1578 under ANDREW MELVILLE (1545-1622). It determined that the government of the Church of Scotland should be Presbyterian. It sanctioned the *Second Book of Discipline* and instructed that presbyteries should be erected throughout Scotland. The Assembly agreed that bishops should be called by their own names and that the title 'bishop' and his authority should be banished from Scotland.

The Magdalen Chapel, today in the process of renovation and restoration, was the first place where the Reformed faith was proclaimed in September 1556. John Craig, shortly after 1560, preached in Latin because he had forgotten Scots! It is rightly called the 'Cradle of the Reformation in Scotland' and is also of historical importance to Baptists and the Edinburgh Medical Missionary Society.

METHODISTS

JOHN WESLEY (1703-91), who often visited Edinburgh, made this note on Sunday 28th May 1786:

> *I preached first in our own house and at noon on the Castle Hill. I never saw such a congregation there before. But the chair was placed just opposite to the sun. I soon forgot it while I expanded the words, 'I saw the dead, small and great, stand before God'. In the evening the whole audience seemed to feel 'without holiness, no man shall see the Lord ....'*

In 1801 Thomas Preston, a Methodist probationer, wrote:

The greatest bar which prevents Methodism from prospering in this country is the Doctrines of Calvin being nearly universally received, so that as soon as a general salvation is offered, we are looked upon as deceivers of the people, and many to this day believe the Methodists to be the false prophets mentioned in Scripture. At present, salvation is seldom heard in the churches, the Gospel being preached rather as a system of doctrines, than as truths which are to be experienced.

Edmund Grindrod, a minister, led a revival in 1826 at the Methodist Chapel in Nicolson Square:

Upon the Quarterly Fast Day, October 6th, our prayer meetings were unusually well attended in the evening. I judge by a moderate calculation three hundred were present. A most solemn and overwhelming sense of the presence of God pervaded the Assembly and shortly it was perceptible that many souls were in deep distress. There was not the slightest confusion. The whole meeting seemed to be dissolved in tears, and the cries of the penitents in subdued but very affecting tones were heard in many parts of the large room in which we were met.

OLD ST PAUL'S

There was always a close connection between Scottish Episcopacy and the Jacobites. Old St Paul's was for long a centre of intrigue for exiled Stuart sympathisers. When Episcopacy was abolished, Bishop Rose, with those who recognised James VIII, worshipped in a wool-store at Carrubber's Close until 1788, when Prince Charles Stuart died. Previously the building had been the residence of Jacobite SIR ROBERT SIBBALD (1641-1722), first Professor of Medicine.

Bonnie Prince Charlie's doctor on the Jacobite march to Derby and at the battle of Culloden, SIR STUART THREIPLAND (1716-1805), presided at vestry meetings. Sir Stuart arranged for the chapel to be used by Thomas Sheridan (father of the dramatist) for lectures in elocution. He also helped WILLIAM GED (1690-1749), a printer and inventor of the stereotype, who was a Jacobite and office-bearer at the chapel.

Isabella Lumisden, a member of the congregation at Old St Paul's, made it a condition of marriage to her suitor, Sir Robert Strange, that he fight for the Young Pretender. This he did – at Prestonpans and Falkirk – and he also engraved banknotes for Prince Charles.

THOMAS RUDDIMAN (1674-1757), printer, grammarian, Keeper of the Advocates Library and owner of the Jacobite paper, *The Caledonian Mercury*, was also a member of the chapel. In the nineteenth century, the songwriter Baroness Nairne was a seat-holder.

Alexander Campbell, singing-master to Sir Walter Scott, played the organ there in 1782. There was a story told how Campbell came to Walter Scott's house in George Square one day to conduct a singing lesson. Scott (who was himself once an Episcopalian) recalled that his 'neighbour, Lady Cumming, sent to beg that the boys might not all be flogged precisely at the same hour, as the noise was really dreadful'!

From 1745-92 Episcopalians were severely

penalised. For a period the chapel was closed and its members met in their own homes.

An interesting link with America came in 1784 when a former Edinburgh medical student, SAMUEL SEABURY (1729-96) from Connecticut, was consecrated bishop. There were no bishops at that time in America and only those who acknowledged the royal supremacy (unlike the American separatists) could be ordained in England.

After the death of Prince Charles Edward Stuart, the Episcopalians reluctantly acknowledged the Hanoverian king. Nevertheless, at Old St Paul's, Alexander Halket used to read the responses from an ancient prayer book which contained the names of Charles II, the Duke of York and Princess Anne. When the name of King George was read, Halket blew his nose loudly enough to drown the reference.

ST ANDREW'S, GEORGE STREET

This was the only church in Edinburgh to be designed by a soldier, Major Frazer (who also constructed Fort George near Inverness).

One minister, David Ritchie, preached on Sundays and also lectured at the University in Logic. Sir Robert Christison remembered him as 'a tall, big-boned strong man with a powerful rough voice, and great energy, but with little polish in his delivery'.

On 18th May 1843 Professor David Welsh, Moderator of the last Assembly, read in St Andrew's the 'Protest of Commissioners to the General Assembly', signed by 203 ministers and elders, proclaiming the right to secede from what they saw as an unscriptural establishment.

The Free Church of Scotland was born

when 451 ministers (out of 1200) resigned from the Church of Scotland in what has become known as the 'Disruption'.

Included among many famous names were **DR THOMAS CHALMERS** (1780-1847) and **DR THOMAS GUTHRIE** (1803-73). Lord Cockburn wrote:

They walked in procession down Hanover Street where they had secured an excellent hall, through an unbroken mass of cheering people, and beneath innumerable handkerchiefs waving from the windows. But amidst this exultation there was much sadness and many a tear, many a grave face and fearful thought ....

DR THOMAS CHALMERS *(above) and* DR THOMAS GUTHRIE

At Edinburgh University two out of three professors and 93 students in the Divinity Faculty resigned. In 1846 the foundation-stone of New College was laid by Dr Thomas Chalmers and a chair of Biblical Criticism established at Edinburgh University.

In the 1875 edition of the *Encyclopaedia Britannica*, a former student at New College, William Smith, shocked the Evangelical wing of the Church by backing the theory of the multiple authorship of the Pentateuch. Six years later he was dismissed by the General Assembly.

ST CUTHBERT'S

During Cromwell's attack on Edinburgh Castle in 1650, the kirk session could not meet because 'there lay a company of soldiers in the church'.

After the battle of Dunbar, Oliver Cromwell set up one of his batteries in the church.

The church was 'altogether spoiled, neither pulpit, loft nor seat left therein, neither door, window nor glass'. The roof was riddled with cannon and musket shot.

Ten years later, under the Episcopal regime, the ministers and flock of St Cuthbert's were ejected.

David Williamson, the minister, who had commanded a part of the Covenanting army at Bothwell Bridge, was imprisoned in the Tolbooth. Known as 'Dainty David' because of his refined tastes, Williamson was the first man in Scotland to wear a watch and he had had seven wives!

One of the most spirited uses of irony took place at St Cuthbert's in 1745. The **REVD NEIL MCVICAR**, a suburban clergyman, apparently unflustered by nearby Jacobite forces, informed the commander of the Castle that he intended to conduct services as usual and climbed his pulpit at the hour appointed. Certainly his confidence was boosted by the guns in Edinburgh Castle and by his own Covenanting persuasion. One observer wrote:

The church was filled with a great congregation, among whom he recognised many Jacobites, as well as some Highland soldiers, attracted by the report of his intentions and the reputation he bore for courageous character. He prayed as usual for King George by name, and then added 'Bless the King. Thou knowest what King I mean. As for the man that is come among us seeking an earthly crown, we beseech Thee in mercy to take him to Thyself and give him a crown of glory'. When this was reported to Prince Charles, he is said to have laughed, and expressed himself highly pleased at the courage and charity of the minister.

John Wesley, in his *Journal*, describes a Sunday in May 1764 when he attended a Communion service at St Cuthbert's: 'How much more simple, as well as more solemn, is the service of the Church of England.'

The Very Revd Dr James Macgregor once recalled, 'in a high pulpit like that of the old St Cuthbert's, I sometimes suffered from a nervous feeling the moment I closed my eyes in prayer, a feeling as if the pulpit and occupant were sinking together'.

Inside the church there were 'petty galleries stuck up one above another, to the very rafters, like so many pigeons' nests'. The church was in a ruinous state, damaged by the Duke of Gordon's cannon when he defended the city for James VII in 1689. One Sunday in September 1772, a gallery cracked, causing a stampede.

ST GEORGE'S, CHARLOTTE SQUARE

The artist and critic JOHN RUSKIN (*circa* 1819-1900) described it as 'a most costly and ugly building' when it opened on 5th June 1814.

One minister, ANDREW THOMSON, improved Scottish psalmody with the help of his choirmaster R A SMITH (who also wrote the music for 'Jessie the flow'r o' Dunblane').

The choirmaster from 1870-81 was SIR A C MACKENZIE (1847-1935), later Principal of the Royal Academy of Music in London.

The eccentric John Sheriff, 'Dr Syntax' in Crombie's *Modern Athenians*, boasted he had listened to more than 300 courses of lectures. He attended St George's often, standing in the front gallery with ink-horn, pen and note book in which he sketched the preacher. When he died, Sheriff was buried at Warriston Cemetery with the epitaph: 'Erected by those who mourn the loss of Syntax.'

ST GILES

The wooden statue of St Giles (which took pride of place in the church) mysteriously disappeared one July night in 1557. John Knox commented, 'in Edinburgh was that great idol called Saint Giles first drowned in the North Loch, after burned, which raised no small trouble in the Town'.

The Archbishop of St Andrews immediately issued an injunction to have the statue replaced in time for the saint's day on 1st September. But the Town appealed against this decision and went on, five years later, to cut the figure of St Giles out of the City flag,

The LANTERN *and* TOWER *of* ST GILES

replacing it with a thistle. However, the Canongate deer which originally accompanied the saint was left intact on the City arms.

Some of those who had embraced the Reformed faith were later persuaded to renounce it and walk in penance in the annual St Giles procession. But as dignitaries and penitents processed down the High Street, the crowd round about erupted. The penitents were quickly spirited into the crowd and the ranks of the clergy broken.

John Knox writes of St Giles Day:

> *A small grotesque idol was borrowed from the Grey Friars. It was fast fixed with iron nails upon a barrow. There assembled priests, friars, and canons with tabors* [drums] *and trumpets, banners and bagpipes.*
>
> *One began to cry 'Down with the idol; down with it' and without delay it was pulled down. One took him by the heels and dadding his head on the causeway, left Dagon without head or hands.*

On 29th June 1559 the army of the Lords of the Congregation entered Edinburgh.

Some time afterwards the relic of St Giles was apparently taken out of its silver reliquary and deposited in the safe-keeping of the Dean of Guild. The diamond from the ring on the statue's finger was later sold and the arm bone buried in the church.

In 1554, however, an arm bone had been presented to St Giles in Bruges, Belgium. A letter was written in the nineteenth century to the Bishop of Bruges by the Roman Catholic Archbishop Smith of Edinburgh, asking for information about the relic. The reply described the relic as being a *left* arm bone. When

William Chambers was restoring the church in the 1880s, an arm bone was found under the flooring of the area given over to the Dean of Guild. It was thought to be the arm bone of St Giles. It was also, however, a *left* arm bone.

Although John Knox was appointed sole minister at St Giles, his place was from time to time taken by a former Franciscan friar, John Wyllok (like Knox, a powerful preacher). As the Church of England's *Book of Common Prayer* was used, the preacher had to be escorted by a bodyguard to and from the church because of hostility towards the Reformers.

Mary Queen of Scots continued to have mass celebrated at Holyrood. Some of her French soldiers even had the habit of entering St Giles to interrupt the sermon and upset the preachers.

Then, for five months, the Reformers were expelled and Roman Catholic ritual reintroduced with the help of the Bishop of Amiens who had accompanied the military reinforcements from France.

On 14th July 1559 the monasteries of the Dominicans (Blackfriars) and the Franciscans (Greyfriars) 'were demolished and casten down all utterly and all the chapels and colleges around the burgh with their yards were similarly destroyed'. St Giles was pillaged and its altars destroyed. Jewels, silver vessels and vestments were sold by order of the magistrates and the proceeds used to pay for repairs to the fabric of the church. From that time the church was renamed the High Kirk of Edinburgh.

On 31st March 1560 the Roman Catholic mass was celebrated in St Giles for the last

time. That night the Lords of the Congregation gained access to St Giles, broke down
the altars and removed all traces of Roman
Catholic worship.

William Chambers, writing in 1879,
commented: 'By the help of sailors from Leith,
with ropes and ladders, the altars were taken
down and cleared out. All the gold, silver
and other valuables were carefully catalogued
and secured, as may be seen from existing
town records.'

Ten workmen toiled for nine days to
demolish the high altars and the rood loft,
using a mast from Leith with a cradle and
pulleys. Then the interior of the church was
whitewashed.

After the Reformation, existing parish
churches continued in use. Often the pulpit
was moved to the middle of one of the long
walls, and the chancel abandoned or given to
a local landowner for the use of his family.
Sometimes galleries were erected in the aisles
of the nave. This explains why no new churches
had to be built in Edinburgh until the early
seventeenth century.

The minister in St Giles at this time was
assisted by John Cairns as reader. The
Reformers began to use Knox's new *Book of
Common Order*. Wine, formerly forbidden to the
ordinary people under the Roman Catholic
dispensation, was now freely given at the
Sacrament – which in winter was held as early
as four in the morning.

Knox was minister for twelve years, sometimes preaching daily. He denounced Roman
Catholicism. To Knox one mass 'was more
fearful than if ten thousand armed enemies
were landed in any part of the realm of purpose
to suppress the whole religion'.

Meanwhile Mary of Guise had occupied Edinburgh and Leith. At this time one sympathiser saw Knox demonstrate how 'the voice of one man is able in one hour to put more life in us than five hundred trumpets continually blustering in our ears'.

On 11th June 1560 cannon at Edinburgh Castle announced the death of Mary of Guise. The port of Leith surrendered and a month later France made peace with England. All French and English troops prepared to leave Scotland. Ministers arranged services of thanksgiving in St Giles where John Knox preached from the prophet Haggai on the 'restoration of the Temple'.

JOHN KNOX
and
KNOX'S PULPIT
(*below*)

The *Scots Confession* was approved by Parliament, rejecting the authority and jurisdiction of the Pope. Saying or hearing the mass was made a criminal offence. In spite of this, Archbishop Hamilton and many other priests continued to do so with relative immunity.

However, in 1562, when Knox preached in St Giles, attacking Mary Queen of Scots' mass and the dancing and fiddling at her court, the Queen thought it prudent not to be present.

In 1562 John Craig was appointed Knox's fellow minister at St Giles. Craig had once been suspected of heresy. He went to Italy where he read Calvin's *Institutions* in the library of the Inquisition and became a Protestant.

Although he had left the Dominican Order, he was held on heresy charges. Narrowly avoiding execution in Rome in 1559, he escaped and in

1560 returned to Scotland. In 1561 he became minister of the Canongate. He proclaimed the banns between Queen Mary and Lord James Bothwell, but denounced the marriage. He helped Knox compile the *First Book of Discipline* and was moderator in 1569 and 1581. In 1580 he drew up the National Covenant.

Great upheavals took place at St Giles in 1571 when Sir William of Grange placed a military force on the roof and steeple of the church to defend the cause of Mary Queen of Scots.

The craftsmen of the city broke into the church and threatened, Samson-like, to pull down the central pillars of the building.

On 4th June Kirkcaldy's men made holes in the vaulted ceiling and fired down upon the citizens below – but all in vain.

Changes in worship were equally dramatic. In the 1570s, services in St Giles would begin at nine in the morning and end at two in the afternoon. Three ministers preached one after the other between readings and the singing of psalms.

John Knox died on 24th November 1572 and was buried in St Giles kirkyard. The event was witnessed by Regent Morton, who noted, 'There lies one who neither feared nor flattered any flesh'.

Ten years later the town was divided into four parishes with their own parish kirks – St Giles, the Magdalen Chapel, the New Kirk (St Cuthbert's), Trinity College; plus the Canongate Kirk (for those outside the city ports).

When James VI finally returned to Scotland in 1617, the chapel at Holyrood was re-fitted according to the English liturgical fashion for a service accompanied by an organ and the singing of a male choir. A banqueting-house was built at the back of St Giles, where the King was entertained with food, wine and festivities.

Just before Christmas 1618 the King tried to ensure that on Yule Day all ministers would preach on the subject of Christ's birth. The people were lukewarm about this and St Giles was half-filled, with dogs running over the floor of the deserted church.

Fifteen years later confrontation came to a head when James' son, King Charles I, arrived in Edinburgh.

Edinburgh was erected into a bishopric later that year — St Giles became a cathedral church with the principal minister as dean and the other ministers in Edinburgh as prebendaries (honorary canons).

The King brought with him the future Archbishop of Canterbury, William Laud, who entered St Giles without warning. The Protestant reader was removed and replaced by two English chaplains in white surplices, who assisted the Bishop in the Anglican service.

The King announced that he was about to endow a new bishopric. He held a Parliament and appointed **WILLIAM FORBES** (1585-1634) as Bishop. Forbes was hardly consecrated when he fell ill, died and was buried in St Giles.

On the morning of 23rd July 1637 the reader at St Giles read prayers from the Scottish *Book of Common Order*. At ten o'clock, the Bishop of Edinburgh processed into St Giles with James Hanna, the dean. The dean sat in the reader's seat, facing the Privy Council and the Town Council, and began to read from the new Anglican prayer book.

Immediately there were shouts of 'False anti-Christian', 'beastly belly-god', 'crafty fox' and 'Judas' from the congregation. The Bishop asked the congregation to be silent and told the dean to continue reading.

At this, Jenny Geddes, a vegetable-seller, shouted, *'Deil colic the wame of thee. Out, thou false thief! Dost thou say mass at my lug?'* and hurled the stool she sat on at the Bishop's head. Uproar followed as stools flew through the air. The people were cleared from the church, but the Bishop was attacked and

The FAMOUS STOOL *of* JENNY GEDDES

pelted with rubbish as he ran off. Following this protest the Anglican liturgy was kept out of Edinburgh until almost the nineteenth century.

The year 1638 saw the signing of the National Covenant. Then came the resumption of a presbyterian form of church government in 1639. The old Scots liturgy of morning and evening prayer (which had apparently led to a considerable amount of intemperance) was replaced in 1650 by Bible reading and by preaching.

Astonishment reigned when Oliver Cromwell entered the city after the battle of Dunbar (1650). Many of his army – captains, commanders and troopers – went up into the pulpit to preach, still carrying their swords and pistols. In addition, large numbers of Quakers appeared and interrupted the ministers' sermons. The Quakers acclaimed the descent of the Holy Spirit and waved their hands round in an ecstasy offensive to those of the undemonstrative Presbyterian tradition.

Observance of Christmas was forbidden, the stool of repentance was burned and the king's seat demolished. For six years no communion service was held in St Giles.

After the Restoration of 1660 the Episcopalian order was again established – the Church of Scotland became part-presbyterian and part-episcopalian, with power and responsibility shared between presbytery and bishop. St Giles was renamed a 'cathedral'.

But this compromise did not suit everyone. As the year drew to a close, a sermon was preached in St Giles which lamented 'the corruption of God's worship'.

After the battle of Rullion Green in 1666, Covenanter prisoners were held in St Giles at the tiny Haddo's Hole, almost suffocating for want of air. Most of them were taken off to be tortured or executed. When the Earl of Argyll came to be executed in 1685, his head was placed on a spike at the east gable of the church.

When James VII fled to France in 1688, there were riots in Edinburgh. Roman

The EXECUTION *of the* EARL *of* ARGYLL

Catholic chapels were attacked and the bishops sent the Bishop of Edinburgh, **ALEXANDER ROSE**, to London to secure their interests.

Alexander Rose was the Church of Scotland's last Bishop of Edinburgh. He was appointed in January 1688 and deprived of office in April 1689 when episcopacy was abolished in Scotland. Bishop Rose lived on in Edinburgh until his death in 1720, as priest to the Jacobite congregation at Old St Paul's in Carrubber's Close.

The office of Bishop of Edinburgh nevertheless continued to have considerable political significance. In 1720, for example, Bishop Fullarton was appointed with the approval of the Old Pretender ('James VIII'), who also made him one of his trustees in Scotland.

A most bizarre legal case occurred in 1697 when a student, Thomas Aitkenhead, the son of an Edinburgh apothecary, publicly questioned the doctrine of the Holy Trinity (God as Father, Son and Holy Spirit) and was condemned to death by hanging for the crime of blasphemy.

In the second half of the seventeenth century four separate congregations met in St Giles – the *High* in the choir (for the Lords of Session and Town Council); the *Tolbooth* in the south-western part; the *Old Kirk* in the nave; and the *Little Kirk* in the north-west corner.

The divisions of St Giles served different tastes – the High Kirk was dignified and aristocratic in manner; the Old Kirk suited those who liked direct and well-grounded sermons; while the Tolbooth Kirk sheltered the 'Tolbooth Whigs' from the head of the Bow and the Lawnmarket – fervent Calvinists who preferred inspirational preaching and having the lines of the psalm recited by a precentor before they were sung.

Other parts of the building became a police station, the Town Clerk's office, a grammar school and a weaver's workshop. The site of the former high altar and the south transept became a meeting-place for businessmen to transact their affairs and seal agreements.

But St Giles also continued to be used for great occasions of State. To mark the Treaty of Union in 1707, a solemn service was held in St Giles with a large congregation, many of whom were Members of Parliament.

At this period the *Book of Common Order* had been discarded and prayers were often wild, extempore outpourings – '*O Lord, there are two great beasts in the world: the Turk and the Pope of Rome. Destroy them both and bring down that great enemy of Christ's Kirk, the tyrant of France!*'

There were sometimes dramatic incidents of another kind. In 1736 a condemned criminal was brought to St Giles from the nearby Tolbooth on the Sunday before his execution. The bells were ringing and the doors were open while the people came into the church. The prisoner watched his opportunity and suddenly springing up, got over the pew into the passage that led to the door in Parliament Close and quickly made his escape.

The English journalist and spy **DANIEL DEFOE** (1660-1731) observed that the bells of St Giles, were 'played upon with keys, and by a man's hand, like a harpsichord; the person playing has great strong wooden cases to his fingers by which he is able to strike with more force'.

Following the Jacobite uprising of 1745, ecclesiastical life in Edinburgh remained on a

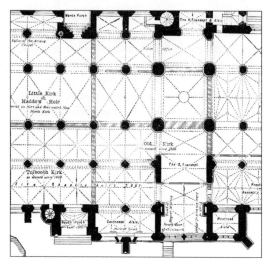

DETAIL *from the* ST GILES PLAN *before the* 1829 ALTERATIONS

relatively even keel. Then, preaching morality in high literary form, **DR HUGH BLAIR** (1718-1800) became minister at St Giles. Blair was an eloquent and stylish preacher admired by Burns. 'I love Blair's sermons,' proclaimed Samuel Johnson after his visit to Edinburgh in 1773, 'though the dog is a Scotchman and a Presbyterian!'

Perhaps the most violent destruction of the fabric of St Giles took place with the well-intentioned 'restoration' of the building in 1829 by the architect William Burn. Lead coffins were removed and sold, tombstones broken up, and cartloads of carved stones taken away, some of which found their way to suburban rockeries. The outside of the church was even faced with paving-stones. When it was finished in 1833 the exterior of the church was ruined and the interior patched and sub-divided into two separate places of worship.

Fortunately, the publisher **LORD PROVOST WILLIAM CHAMBERS** (1800-83) intervened, and in February 1879 the restoration of St Giles began. When the floor was lifted up, Chambers recalls that 'a hideous scene of decaying mortal remains was disclosed. Thickly beneath the floor lay heaps of skulls and bones in indiscriminate confusion'.

The remains – two tons in weight – were taken to Greyfriars kirkyard and re-interred with due ceremony. By 1883 St Giles was restored to something of its former glory.

ST JOHN'S, CORSTORPHINE

Some churches were a beacon shining in the darkness in more ways than one. Dating from the twelfth century, St John's, Corstorphine had a niche in the east wall of the chancel where a light would be placed to guide pilgrims across the marshes around the church. However, in the eighteenth century the marsh was drained and the guiding light discontinued.

After the battle of Dunbar in 1650 St John's suffered the fate of many churches when Cromwell's troops occupied the building.

In 1672 **GEORGE HENDRY** was inducted as minister. He fought tooth and nail with heritors who were absent from the kirk and accused the local laird of discouraging tenants from attending, from supplying the minister with coal, or working the glebe.

In his *Answer to Scotch Presbyterian Eloquence*, Hendry tells how he found a strange cow in the churchyard. Enraged, 'he ran at her like a bulldog and throwing his Bible at her, wished that all the plagues and curses contained in that book might befall her and her master, that did not keep her better at home'.

ST JOHN'S, PRINCES STREET

When the Episcopal Church was disestablished in 1689, there were almost 600 Episcopalian clergy; two-thirds of the Scottish nation was Episcopalian. The Penal Law against Jacobites and Episcopalians was not repealed until 1792. By then there were only four bishops and around 40 clergy; Episcopalians made up a mere one-twentieth of the Scottish population.

A notable figure at the Charlotte Chapel in West Register Street was **BISHOP DANIEL SANDFORD** (1766-1830), 'a thin pale man, with an air and aspect full of a certain devout and melancholy sort of abstraction and a voice which is very tremulous, yet deep in its tones and managed so as to produce a very striking and impressive effect'.

In 1818, three years after St John's had been constructed, William Burns' open stone lantern at St John's, Princes Street was blown down. The *Scots Magazine* reported that 'all the large and small minarets on the top of St John's Chapel were blown down, leaving the tower a complete ruin. Two of the larger ornaments were carried thirty feet and penetrated not only the roof of the church but also the floor, breaking into the vaults beneath'.

Sir Walter Scott (whose Episcopalian mother was buried at St John's), writing to William Laidlaw, added that 'the devil never so well deserved the title of Prince of the Power of the Air, since he has blown down this handsome church and left the ugly mass of new buildings standing on the North Bridge'.

Perhaps the most celebrated priest at St John's was **DEAN EDWARD RAMSAY** (1793-1872), whose *Reminiscences of Scottish Life and Character* preserved so much of local culture.

ST MARY'S RC CATHEDRAL

In 1879 the Archbishop of Amalfi in Italy sent to Edinburgh what was believed to be the shoulder blade of St Andrew the Apostle. It had been brought to Amalfi after the Fall of Constantinople in 1204.

At St Peter's, Rome in April 1969, Pope Paul VI gave another relic to **CARDINAL GORDON GRAY** (1910-93), at that time also Archbishop of St Andrews and Edinburgh. 'Peter greets his brother Andrew,' were the words of the Pope to the Archbishop. The relics of the Apostle are today displayed at St Andrew's altar in the Metropolitan Cathedral of St Mary.

St Andrew is of special significance to Scots. The 'Declaration of Arbroath' (1320) to Pope John XXII is an appeal to the Vatican against the English claim that Scotland fell within the jurisdiction of the Archbishops of York. The Declaration argues that the Scots are a distinct people who had long enjoyed the protection of St Andrew, brother of St Peter. St Andrew is described in the Declaration of Arbroath as 'our patron or protector'.

ST PATRICK'S

There were two kinds of Episcopalians – those who opposed the Hanoverian dynasty, declined the oaths and worked for the restoration of the Stuarts; and those who 'qualified' by accepting the Revolution, the Church of England's forms of worship and praying for King George.

At first the Episcopalians worshipped in a chapel in Blackfriars Wynd, which the English lexicographer, critic and novelist **SAMUEL JOHNSON** (1709-84) attended in 1773. However, his companion James Boswell noted that the Doctor was inattentive to the sermon – 'Mr Carre's voice not being strong enough to reach his hearing'.

In 1771 the foundation-stone of a new Episcopal chapel was laid by Grand Master Mason Sir James Oughton. The Writers to the Signet contributed 200 guineas and the Incorporation of Surgeons 40 guineas.

Hugo Arnot, the historian, saw its opening in October 1774 as 'a mark of increasing moderation and liberality. Not many years ago, Episcopacy in all its ceremonies would not have been tolerated and the chapel would have fallen a sacrifice to the fury of the mob'.

A concave ceiling on the east side above the altar was decorated by the painter **ALEXANDER RUNCIMAN** (1736-85) with murals of the Ascension, of Christ talking to the Samaritan woman, of the Prodigal returned (based on the features of the poet Robert Fergusson), and figures of Moses and Elias.

In 1799 an Episcopalian clergyman named Fitzsimmons was found guilty at the High Court of helping four French prisoners, who had been arrested as spies, to escape from Edinburgh Castle. They had stayed for five days in Fitzsimmons' house at Chessel's Court. Then he took them to Newhaven where they used a fishing-boat to reach a French vessel lying off Inchkeith. For three months Fitzsimmons was imprisoned in the Canongate Tolbooth.

Archibald Alison, an Episcopalian preacher, was described thus by Lord Cockburn in 1800: 'His voice was clear and sweet, his taste very refined and his air and gesture very polite. It was the poetry of preaching.'

In 1856 the church was re-opened as a

Roman Catholic church (St Patrick's) and is now staffed by priests of the Franciscan Order.

ST TRIDUANA'S, RESTALRIG

On 21st December 1560 the first General Assembly of the Church of Scotland made a decision to transfer the parish church from St Triduana's, Restalrig to Leith and to raze the Chapel Royal at Restalrig to the ground as a place of idolatry.

The roof was taken off and the building pulled down, except for the walls of the chancel and the eastern window. The holy well of St Triduana was filled up.

From 1560-1836 the ruins of the former Chapel Royal were open to the heavens. Then the Restalrig Friendly Society began a restoration of the church which opened for worship the following year.

SOUTH LEITH

Up to the time of the Reformation the parish church of Leith was St Triduana's, Restalrig. A chapel at the Kirkgate in Leith was erected around 1483 and dedicated to the Virgin Mary. In 1544 St Mary's was burned by the Earl of Hertford's army and in 1547 used as a prison. The reformer GEORGE WISHART (1513-46) preached his last recorded sermon there (from the Parable of the Sower) with John Knox in the congregation. Then in 1609 St Mary's, Leith was constituted as the parish church.

The Convention of Leith, held in the church, drew up a concordat between Church and State for a modified form of episcopacy – which was backed by Knox. But this scheme was abandoned when Melville promoted the divine right of Presbytery.

When the National Covenant came to be signed, 'all within the church stood up upon their feet and solemnly with uplifted hands did swear unto the said Covenant'.

After the battle of Dunbar, St Mary's became a military store. Parishioners held open-air services among the ruins of Restalrig.

JOHN LOGAN, minister from 1773-86, published a play, a tragedy entitled 'Runnamede', which was acted in an Edinburgh theatre. However, because of this he was forced to resign by the Kirk authorities and died in London. In 1781 Logan had published poems which included 'Ode to the Cuckoo', called by Edmund Burke 'the most beautiful lyric in our language'.

Another Leith man, **REVD JOHN HOME** (1722-1808), also wrote a play – 'Douglas' – which led to him being suspended by his presbytery.

TRINITY COLLEGE

TRINITY
COLLEGE
COLLEGIATE
SEAL

During the years 1594-5 the Reformed Communion service was celebrated in Trinity College. In 1594 the College was also used for the laureation of students at Edinburgh University in the presence of the Queen and the ambassadors. The College was decorated with flowers; chairs and cushions were brought in for the guests.

By 1726 Trinity College Hospital had become dilapidated – slates were tumbling off the roof, threatening the lives of innocent people walking in the street. The floor in the low gallery (the women's apartments) and the joists were all rotten. Through the north end of the house ran the waters of the Nor' Loch.

Then in 1848 (before the College was finally dismantled to make way for the new North British Railway), a search was made for the body of the founder, Queen Mary of Gueldres. A skeleton was found and buried in the Royal Vault in Holyrood on 15th July.

However, in September 1848 another skeleton was found near the high altar. The archaeologists believed this to be the Queen. These remains were also buried in Holyrood Chapel, but outside the Royal Vault.

THE TRON

Lord Cockburn vividly described the Tron Kirk fire of 16th November 1824 thus:

> *We ran out from the Court, gowned and wigged, and saw that it was the steeple, an old Dutch thing, composed of wood, iron and lead, and edged all the way up with bits of ornament.*
>
> *Some of the sparks the preceding night had nestled in it, and had at last blown its dry bones into flame. There could not be a more beautiful firework; only it was wasted on the day-light. It was one hour's brilliant blaze. The spire was too high and too combustible to admit of any attempt to save it, so we had nothing to do but admire. And it was certainly beautiful.*
>
> *The fire seized on every projecting point, and played with the fret-work as if it had all been an exhibition. The outer covering boards were soon consumed and the lead dissolved.*
>
> *This made the strong upright and cross beams visible; and these stood, with the flame lessened, but with the red fire increased, as if it had been a great burning toy.*

When it was all over, and we were begin-
ning to move back to our clients, Sir Walter
Scott, whose father's pew had been in the Tron
Church, lingered a moment, and said, with a
profound heave, 'Eh, sirs, mony a weary,
weary sermon hae I heard beneath that steeple!'

CARBERRY TOWER

Since 1961 the fifteenth century Carberry
Tower, with its leafy grounds near Musselburgh, has been a unique Church of Scotland
resource for training and personal development. In 1996 the property was taken over as
a conference and retreat centre by The
Carberry Trust, which numbers among its
trustees representatives from the major
Christian denominations.

Carberry takes a special interest in music
and the arts and is committed to the renewal
of church and nation.

Perhaps the notice on Carberry's main
driveway sums up best the welcoming spirit
of the place: 'SLOW – Children and Animals'.

Carberry made a special contribution to
détente when in 1981 it hosted the first of
the 'Edinburgh Conversations' between
British and Russian scientists. There was no
table in the North Library where the
conversations took place. Consequently there
was no head of the table. All were equal.

CHANGES IN PIETY

Changes which affected worship during the
end of the eighteenth century were another
subject acutely observed by Lord Cockburn,
that perceptive chronicler of manners:

As to the comparative religiousness of the present and the preceding generation, any such comparison is very difficult to be made.

Religion is certainly more the fashion than it used to be. There is more to be said about it; there has been a great rise, and consequently a great competition, of sects; and the general mass of the religious public has been enlarged.

On the other hand, if we are to believe one half of what some religious persons themselves assure us, religion is now almost extinct. My opinion is that the balance is in favour of the present time.

MODERN LANDMARKS

In more recent times Edinburgh found itself playing an important role in the history of religion. The 1910 World Missionary Conference, attended by delegates from nearly all the Protestant churches and missionary agencies, was held in Edinburgh, heralding the beginning of what was to be known as the Ecumenical Movement.

Out of the Edinburgh Conference on Faith and Order, emerged the movement of Faith and Order, which held its first conference in 1927 at Lausanne, Switzerland, at which delegates from the Greek Orthodox churches officially met representatives of the West's Protestant churches for the first time.

MIDLOTHIAN
Post-Reformation

COCKPEN

Kirk affairs could be deadly serious. On 2nd May 1708 the Cockpen kirk minister read before the congregation the sentence of excommunication on George Hastie and Margaret Watson for living together while unmarried:

> *Whereas thou have been by sufficient proof convicted of living together in sin, and after one admonition in prayer, remain obstinate without any evidence or sign of true repentance, and do contumaciously resist the authority of the Church, therefore, in the name of the Lord Jesus Christ and before this congregation, I pronounce and declare you excommunicated, shut out from the communion of the faithful; debar you from their privileges and deliver you to Satan for the destruction of thy flesh, that thy spirit may be saved in the day of the Lord Jesus.*

Some alienated themselves from the community in other ways. About 150 yards west of Cockpen school is 'Curlie's Corner', after curly-haired Sandy Arthur who was buried there. He hanged himself in May 1814 from a wooden beam at a coal pit south of Bonnyrigg. As suicides could not be buried in a churchyard, his body was put into a grave dug on the boundary line between the Dalhousie and Polton estates.

Yet a minister's life could also have its innocent distractions. Perhaps the **REVD JAMES GRIERSON MD** (ordained 1844) sometimes wished *he* could bury himself out of public sight. Instead he left to posterity a worthy tome entitled *Observations on the Natural History and Habits of the Mole.*

FALA

An amusing incident occurred at Fala in 1880. James Duncan, the headmaster, records:

> *On the south side of the church lay the old graveyard safe – a huge cumbersome iron construction which, when put over a grave, must have been difficult to remove. But finally it disappeared and it was generally supposed that it had been broken up and carted off for old iron.*
>
> *There was a Committee of Watchers who, in twos and threes, patrolled the churchyard at nights, armed with a blunderbuss. But in spite of the safe and the watchmen, there were at least two cases of body-snatching.*
>
> *Once the Watchers thought they had done a great deed. In the darkness they had fired on and scared off what they conceived to be graveyard thieves, but next morning it was found that the minister's goat had been badly wounded!*

NEWBATTLE

At the time of the Reformation in 1560 Mark Ker was made commendator (administrator). The Lordship of Newbattle was later conferred on his son. Shortly after, the Abbey and church were demolished.

Newbattle had some political importance in the years that followed. After his execution in 1661, the body of the Marquis of Argyle lay in the Newbattle vault for two months under the care of the Earl of Lothian.

NEWTON

Ingenious strategies were devised to allow true love to prosper between lovers who were not both members of the Church of Scotland.

Around the year 1630 Lord Linton and Lady Seton were illegally joined in a mixed marriage at Newton church.

The key had been given to Lady Elibank of the Drum and on a Sunday evening in winter, while the resident minister was away in Dalkeith, the ceremony was performed.

But church life was not always convenient. In the same century, Lady Melrose of Sheriff-hall complained to the Presbytery of Dalkeith that the ladder to the pillar of repentance obstructed her view of the minister. So the ladder was quickly removed and a new entry made from outside the church.

PENICUIK

Some of the ministers of Penicuik were far from being models of propriety. In 1605 the former minister of Penicuik, **WILLIAM GALBRAITH**, was convicted for perjury before the Lords of Council and Session and sentenced to be taken to the market cross of Edinburgh. There he was made to stand for the space of an hour with a paper on his head, containing in great letters the words 'Mansworne, perjured, infamous'. Then he was banished from Britain for ever.

Others had laughable weaknesses, such as **THOMAS COLSTON** who was ordained minister for Penicuik in 1799. He constantly chewed tobacco and was evidently a conceited man.

On one occasion he was in the home of a prominent citizen when one of the younger members of the household decided to teach the minister a lesson. He began to praise the minister's beautifully formed features, running his finger along the minister's brow, cheeks and nose. But the boy had previously dipped his finger in a sticky black substance and, after the eulogising, the minister's face was covered in black!

Shortly before he died in 1829, Colston gave the order that the following inscription should be placed above his grave: *'Here lies the rare T.C.'*

There were other comic incidents, like the one that took place with the early nineteenth century Watch Committee who patrolled with two guns to protect the cemetery from resurrectionists.

One of them, Henry Dewar, heard something moving about the tombs and, thinking it was a grave-robber, loosed off his gun. When the Watch Committee got to the intruder, they found they had shot a pig!

In the same period, the dissenting Burgher congregation at Brigend had as their minister the **REVD PATRICK COMRIE**, a man with a great sense of humour.

Once a certain Thomas Wilkie was up for election as an elder. One of the congregation remarked that Wilkie had a saintly wife and a God-fearing family. Mr Comrie replied:

If his saintly wife and God-fearing family could be made elders, I would not wag my tongue against them. But Mr Wilkie himself is a curly-wurly conglomerate of good and evil, every

*Sunday in the kirk listening to the sermon and
singing psalms like a perfect saint, while on
the weekdays he is at the markets and fairs
lying and cheating like the biggest swindler!*

After the Napoleonic Wars there was a
large influx of Roman Catholics into Penicuik,
in the form of French prisoners of war.

The publisher William Chambers visited
Valleyfield prisoner of war depot when he
was a young man:

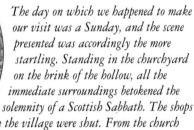

WILLIAM
CHAMBERS

*The day on which we happened to make
our visit was a Sunday, and the scene
presented was accordingly the more
startling. Standing in the churchyard
on the brink of the hollow, all the
immediate surroundings betokened the
solemnity of a Scottish Sabbath. The shops
in the village were shut. From the church
was heard the voice of the preacher. Looking
down from the height on the hive of living
beings, there was not among them a vestige of
the ordinary calm of Sunday – only Dimanche!
Dressed in coarse woolen clothing of a yellow
colour, and most of them wearing red or blue
cloth caps, or partly-coloured cowls, the prisoners
were engaged in a variety of amusements and
occupations. Prominently, and forming the
centre of attraction, were a considerable number
ranked up in two rows, joyously dancing to the
sound of a fiddle, which was briskly played by
a man who stood on the top of a barrel. Others
were superintending cookery in big pots over
open fires, which they fanned by the flapping
of cocked hats. Others were fencing with sticks
amidst a circle of eager onlookers.*

PENTLAND

Four miles from Rullion Green (where the people of Pentland were defeated by General Tam Dalyell), many Covenanters were buried in Old Pentland kirkyard.

The first Reformed Presbyterian church in Scotland was at Pentland where the **REVD JAMES RENWICK** was minister (1683-88). He held *conventicles* (field-preachings) until he was executed in Edinburgh on 17th February 1688.

While in prison, **HELEN ALEXANDER** (a Covenanter from Old Pentland whom James Renwick had married to James Currie, a merchant from Pentland) records: 'I went and saw him in prison. When discoursing about several things, I said, "Sir, within a little you will get the white robes"; he added, "and palms in my hands". And when Renwick was executed, I went along to the Greyfriars churchyard, took him into my arms until stripped of his clothes, helped to wind him in his grave clothes, and helped to put him into his coffin.' James Renwick was the last Covenanter to be executed; he was only 26 years of age.

Helen Alexander also seems to have been the moving spirit behind the 'Children's Bond or Charter' in which some children in Pentland got together in 1683, entering into a solemn league and covenant. The first child to sign was 10 year old Beatrix Umpherston, who later married the Covenanting minister of Loanhead. She lived to be 90 and is buried with her husband in Pentland kirkyard.

The Charter read:

This is a Covenant made between the Lord and us, with our whole hearts, and to give up ourselves freely to Him, without reserve, soul and body, hearts and affections, to be his children, and Him to be our God and Father, if it please the holy Lord to send His gospel to the land again: that we stand to this Covenant which we have written, as we shall answer at the great day ....

ROMAN CAMP HILL

Margaret Hawthorn, known locally as 'Camp Meg', lived on Roman Camp Hill early in the 1800s. She dressed in man's clothing and wellington boots. Armed with a scythe or a sickle, she rode astride her white mare Skewball to all the fairs and races.

The impression she gave was uncanny – she had a slight beard and whiskers, and she lived alone with her Bible and her dog.

Boys who came to visit her were put through the Shorter Catechism. She declared she had seen the Devil and 'thocht him the ugliest brute she had ever seen'. Camp Meg died in 1827.

RULLION GREEN

Nine hundred Covenanters from Galloway faced a Royalist army of 3000 under General Tam Dalyell on 28th November 1666 at Rullion Green in the Pentland Hills, south of Edinburgh.

When defeat finally came, the Covenanter prisoners were taken to Edinburgh – ten were hanged on one gibbet. Others were taken home and hanged in front of their own people. Most were sentenced to be deported to

Barbados. Some were tortured to death.

A century and a half later *Blackwood's Magazine* records a touching story:

> *An enterprising youth, a farmer's son in the Eason district* [near Dunsyre] *went to the top of the hill with a spade with a view to discovering whether tradition was correct in declaring that this spot was the Covenanter's grave. He began to dig and speedily found what he was after. He came home in triumph with a skull, some pieces of cloth and a few brass buttons, but his father, a true-blue Presbyterian, indignant at the desecration of a spot hallowed to the mind of every patriotic Scotsman, first administered a severe thrashing to his son, and then went with him to reinter the sacred relics. It was then resolved to mark the spot with a permanent monument which was placed there in 1841.*

The BATTLE *of* RULLION GREEN

WEST LOTHIAN
Post-Reformation

CONVENTICLES

The Bathgate Hills provided ideal cover for open-air conventicles, where lookouts could warn the faithful by imitating the cry of the curlew or the peewit.

MUCKLE JOCK GIBB from Bo'ness, a fundamentalist preacher, was the leader of a group of women, the *Sweet Singers*, who sang psalms wherever they went. They believed Muckle Jock was the descendant of King Solomon. But Gibb was arrested and flogged in Linlithgow and eventually transported to the West Indies for saying that it was wrong to pay taxes, as all offerings should be made to God alone.

GENERAL TAM DALYELL of the Binns (*circa* 1615-85), a local landowner, campaigned against the Covenanters. They claimed he had the Devil on his side; they believed that water boiled in his riding-boots and bullets bounced off his armour. He was said to have roasted some Covenanters to death in the huge oven at the Binns kitchen and to have been the first to torture them with thumbscrews. (Dalyell = Devil!) But the Devil was said to have been so annoyed with Dalyell that he threatened to blow the Binns down. So Dalyell built the turrets to make the house more secure.

GENERAL
TAM DALYELL
of the BINNS

Dalyell and the Devil were said to play cards every night. Once, when he lost, the Devil is supposed to have thrown the heavy marble card-table out of the house. Later it was found in a nearby pond.

Dalyell changed the uniform of the regiment he had raised (The Royal Scots Dragoon Guards) from red to grey (The Royal Scots Greys), substituting grey Flanders cloth to camouflage them from the Covenanters.

But Dalyell was also a man of honour. He resigned after the Battle of Rullion Green in 1666 because, against his orders, women and children had been killed.

ALEXANDER KIRKWOOD, master in the Grammar School, records how in 1679 he tried to help the 1200 Covenanter prisoners held in Linlithgow:

From 3 in the morning until 10 in the forenoon, I alone stood on the Fleshmarket wall and gave in over it above 300 suits of cloth and exceeding much meat and drink, not without hazard to my person, being often like to follow the cord with which I let down the barrels to the prisoners, of whom many thereafter came back and thanked me heartily for the favour I had done them.

Later, Kirkwood was called before the Provost and town councillors whom he named the 'Twenty-Seven Gods of Linlithgow' in a satirical pamphlet. The Provost ordered Kirkwood to attend Presbyterian services. Kirkwood refused and was dismissed from his post. However, he appealed and in 1712 the Privy Council ruled in his favour. He received damages and expenses from Linlithgow.

Among Kirkwood's pupils were John,

Earl of Stair, and Colonel James Gardiner of Burnfoot near Carriden, who appears in Sir Walter Scott's 'Waverley' novels (*see* pp 38-39).

ALEXANDER REID (*b* 1646), a Covenanter from Bathgate, describes how, around 1665, he was converted:

> *That summer I could work little or none, but lying here and there in the fields, wrestling on the ground, mightily straitened in prayer many times, I would fain look after the Lord.*
>
> *I continued in so sad a condition, that I cannot express the soul-anguish I was in, till about Martinmas following, when the Lord had compassion upon the wretched infant, and took me up.*
>
> *And behold, it was the time of love. He cast his skirts over me and entered into covenant with me, that I should be His. And I thought I did enter into a covenant with Him, so that I got my heart poured out before Him with tears, and made a bargain with Him, covenanting with Him to be His fully, without reservation, committing my soul and body to Him.*

CAPT CREICHTON has left a vivid account of the campaign against the Covenanters. A trooper in the Lifeguards quartered at Bathgate, Creichton describes how he went out one Sunday on the moors with a comrade, to try to find any 'Wanderers', as the Covenanters were sometimes called. The troopers set out disguised as farm labourers, in grey coats and bonnets. After a walk of 10 miles they saw three men armed with long poles on the top of a hill. They recognised them as lookouts.

Coming up slowly and carefully behind the lookouts, Creichton and his companion snatched one of the men's poles and, asking him why he was carrying such a pole on the Lord's Day, suddenly knocked him down. Creichton's comrade captured another. The third man ran off to raise the alarm, but Creichton pursued and overpowered him also.

By this time they knew where the conventicle was from the powerful voice of the preacher which could be heard a quarter of a mile away. But when they reached the conventicle, the troopers found themselves heavily outnumbered. Somehow they managed to seize a horse and escape.

LINLITHGOW

On 29th June 1559 the Lords of the Congregation demolished the altars and holy water stoops and every statue of every saint in St Michael's Church, Linlithgow. St Michael's statue was the only one that survived, because to remove it would have caused structural damage to the building.

The changes in church services were marked. Masses had been relatively quick and there was a stone seat round the outside wall of the church for those who could not stand. Lengthy Protestant services, on the other hand, with their long sermons, needed pews.

Now that candles were no longer used, each trade guild was required to pay for the light from windows. Guilds had to pay for the maintenance of the glass, so some windows were simply built up with stone to save expense.

More energetic times came with the Restoration in 1660. One account stated:

> *After public service the streets were filled with bonfires on both sides, that it was not without hazard to be among them.*

The Earl of Linlithgow came with the magistrates to the Mercat place accompanied with many other gentlemen, where a table was covered with confections. There they were met with the curate of the place, Ramsay (now Bishop of Dunkeld), who prayed and sang a psalm. Then, eating some of the confections, they threw the rest among the people, the fountain all this time running with French wine of several colours and Spanish wine, and continued two or three hours.

His Lordship, with the magistrates and gentlemen, drank the King and Queen's and all the Royal family's healths, breaking baskets of glasses.

At the Mercat Cross was erected a crown standing on an arch on four pillars. On one side of the arch was placed a statue in the form of an old hag having the Covenant in her hands with this superscription: 'A GLORIOUS REFORMATION'.

When the poet **ROBERT BURNS** visited St Michael's, he observed: 'A pretty good old Gothic church. What a poor business is a Presbyterian place of worship, dirty, narrow, squalid. The famous stool of repentance, in the old Roman way, is in a lofty situation.'

DOROTHY WORDSWORTH, some years later, added this comment: 'The shell of a small, ancient church is standing, into which are crammed wooden pews, galleries and pulpit – very ugly and discordant with the exterior.'

LIVINGSTON

JAMES WADDEL (*b circa* 1658), returning from a meeting of Covenanters on the morning of

20th July 1721, walked into a clump of willows beside the Boxton Burn, near Avonbridge. He records: 'Before I left the spot, the Lord was pleased to pity and help and I got there what I resolved never to discover in the world.' Later he added of the incident that 'I not only found Him, but I saw Him whom my soul loved in that bush of willows'.

MIDCALDER

At Tarneymon the famous witches of Calder were believed to have ascended to the moon, flying on broomsticks. Up they went to 'tame' or turn the moon each 28 days, fearing that under the influence of the new calendar of 1582 the moon would go wrong and forget to re-appear in the heavens.

In 1720 JOHN WILKIE, minister of Uphall, was sent to Midcalder church to preach a sermon on witchcraft and to exorcise the spirits there. He preached on a Fast-day, Thursday 14th January, from the text James 4:7 – 'Submit yourselves therefore to God. Resist the devil and he will flee from you.'

What the effect of his sermon was on the Calder witches (which for long had troubled a number of the neighbouring parishes) will never be known.

One of the witches, Ellen Fogo, confessed to having practised black magic on the son of Lord Torphichen.

After they were arrested and imprisoned, some of the witches were burned on the Cunnigar of Midcalder (the witches' knowe), a pre-historic fort between the River Almond and the village.

TORPHICHEN

At the time of the Disruption in May 1843, the minister at Torphichen, the **REVD W HETHERINGTON**, wrote this poignant note to his wife: 'My own beloved and disinherited wife, the deed has been done! We are now sitting in the hall of our new Assembly with feelings of the deepest solemnity and yet holy joy and unutterable peace.'

Within six weeks, on 6th August, the first Free Kirk in Scotland had been built at Torphichen and opened for public worship.

UPHALL

During the tenure of John Wilkie at Uphall, the Secession (later known as the United Presbyterian) Church swept through Linlithgowshire, the first congregation being in the hills at Craigmailen, between Bathgate and Linlithgow.

Seceders came from as far as South Queensferry, Bo'ness, Midcalder and Douglas. In wintertime, before their meeting-house was built, when the snow was falling, the men would take off their large Kilmarnock bonnets and put their feet into them for warmth, wrapping their plaids over their heads. In this condition they would sit on the hillside, listening to the preacher for several hours at a time.

DAVID URE, minister at Uphall from 1796, was deeply interested in geology and botany. We are told that on his expeditions in the district he often carried bread and cheese in his pocket and enjoyed his repast beside the cooling spring. His greatcoat was furnished with a large pocket to store minerals and other curiosities. He carried a tin box for stowing curious plants, a large cudgel armed with steel to serve both as a spade and pickaxe, a few small chisels and other tools, a blow-pipe, a small liquid chemical apparatus and optical instruments. His friends referred to him as 'The Walking Laboratory'.

PART II
Modern Times

In what is sometimes described as a post-Christian society, perhaps the two most important questions to be answered today are: First, where is God to be found in the world around you? And second, what is God's attitude to homelessness, poverty, unemployment, AIDS, and drug-addiction?

In the next part of this book, there follow the answers which men and women in the Lothians today have offered to these questions.

Every religion, denomination or support-group has its own view, but when faced with these fundamental questions, there turns out to be a very large area of common ground.

HINDU

Mr Amrit Lal
PRESIDENT
Hindu Temple, Edinburgh

I believe in Hinduism, but I also look at other
religions in the same way as I look at my own.

I think that God in Edinburgh is the same
as God everywhere. We live in a different
environment to India. We haven't brought a
Hindu God to Edinburgh – God is the same
for everybody. What Hindus have brought
here are different ways of praying, different
aspects of religion that we perform. In the
final analysis there is one supreme power that
we call God.

My personal view is that there is some kind
of supreme power controlling this universe,
without which this universe would not exist.
There is a Creator and I believe in that creative
power. Some call it Lord Krishna, some call it
Lord Rama, some see it through Lord Jesus. I
say that we are looking at one thing and that
is God. It doesn't matter *how* we see it; eventually we all end up at the same point.

I have a very strong faith in religion and in
God. I have been to some extent instrumental
in setting up a Hindu Temple in Edinburgh.
I think this is my small contribution towards
my faith. So I hope I will get a few more
years to complete this project which started
about twelve years ago. I will be very pleased

if I can see it finished in its final form.

There are different windows, you can say. We are looking through different windows which have got different shapes. What we see through these windows is *one* thing, that is God. We are always trying to reach that God and that God has no shape or description; at the same time it can have all the shapes that you want to see. We don't know the sex of God – female or male. But then again, you can say, that the supreme power can take any shape. It can turn into male, female or any shape that we see around us.

So, I think the best way to tell any European why people believe, is that somehow – from their parents or from their forefathers – they have started believing in a certain form and they continue to do so. But that is immaterial – the final thing is that one supreme power. That is what we should be thinking about.

Don't think that our faith is only in a picture or statue. It's not that. It goes much beyond. It goes right up to God.

However, a picture or statue does help us to concentrate. If we have to solve a problem (say, for example, a mathematical problem) we prepare a model. Why do we have to do this? Because we think we can understand the actual problem through the model. So I say, there's a God, but this is simply a model of that God and we're looking at that model; trying to understand that supreme power through this model. That model can take any shape. It can be a picture of Lord Rama, Lord Krishna, even (in Christianity) just a cross or a statue of the Virgin Mary. These are models of something which we are trying to understand.

God is undescribable. He can have any

shape and he can have no shape. You can
choose your models but you cannot choose
God, because that is the supreme power. That
is my understanding of God. God is what is
controlling the whole universe, a universe
where we cannot conceive how it starts and
how it ends. The human brain just cannot
conceive that power of the universe.

If I have a problem, if I am facing difficult
times, I put my full faith in God and that
helps me to relax and to surmount any of my
problems, purely through my faith in God. I
say 'God will help me'.

God is not in the Hindu Temple and the
Temple is not a God. In Hinduism one thing
is important: you can pray at home but it
carries more power if you are sitting in a
gathering and remembering God together. It
has got more impact. This is what Hindu
philosophy says: 'You can (as Lord Buddha
did) pray as an individual, but if you are in a
community, that carries more weight.'

We come together. We recite hymns and
what we call *bhajans*. This has many aspects to
it, but getting people together and singing
together does have more impact on your faith
or your belief. God likes it as well.

Hinduism has a very strong social message
– that we should work towards equality. The
one very strong message is that you must try
to help the poor, the destitute or any person
who is suffering.

In one of our *bhajans* there are the lines,
'If you see a poor or destitute person who is
needing help, try to help that person, male
or female, because you never know but you
might be seeing God – that may be God
testing you in that shape'.

That means that God may have come down

in a shape which you don't recognise. Try to help that person, because you may be facing God there, you may be seeing God. You can never know in what shape you see God.

Hinduism has this insight to offer – don't look at any other religion in a prejudiced way. Simply look and say: 'Yes. Any other religion is as good as my own religion. It's just a different way to look at God.'

Sometimes people come to my door preaching Christianity. On one occasion I brought them in, asked them to sit down and listened to what they said. Then I asked them, 'Do you pray at home?'

'Yes.'

'Have you ever looked at my religion? You are Christians. I am listening to you and you are explaining to me. Perhaps I know a little more about Christianity than you know about Hinduism. I look at different religions in the same way as my own religion.'

I said, 'I'll show you some examples'.

I've got a little prayer-corner in my house. I've got pictures of Lord Krishna and Lord Rama. To prove that I believe equally in Christianity, there's a picture of Jesus Christ in my Temple. I showed it to them:

'I didn't know you were coming. There is the picture of Jesus Christ. I look at all these things. I give them my full respect, the same respect as I give to my own faith.'

They were a bit surprised.

When I was in Singapore, I went to a house which was given to us by the polytechnic where I was teaching engineering. We moved into the empty house. There was nothing there, apart from this picture of Jesus Christ on the wall. So it hit me, 'Look, there's God here, welcoming us to this house'. So we carried that picture with us ever since. This was thirty years ago and it is always in our Temple at home.

But God is not a piece of paper or a statue.

Hell and Heaven are on this earth. If you are living a life of poverty or suffering on earth, Hinduism says that these sufferings are because of deeds you performed in a previous life. So you are paying for them now. It cannot be helped. People who are living very good lives with plenty of money are getting rewards for what good they did in their last life.

The philosophy of Hinduism is, 'Do good deeds all the time, without looking for reward and the reward will eventually come. It is up to God when it will come. It may be late, but it will definitely come.'

DALITS

Mr Alan Mair
ROMAN CATHOLIC THEOLOGIAN
Hostel Supervisor for the Homeless

There is a great tendency within the Church to spiritualise the message, the preaching and teaching of Jesus. In particular, the Gospel passage on Jesus' mission, where Luke starts off by saying, 'I came to give sight to the blind, to set prisoners free'. There is a great over-spiritualisation of that message, instead of trying to understand what Jesus was saying – and what he was saying was very radical. In giving sight to the blind, he was not talking about miracles, returning the actual sight – he was talking about freeing those who are captive, freeing those who are refugees from their oppressors. Taking that as a basis, I would see that God is in and with the minds and hearts of those who suffer.

One of the difficulties I have is to go to Mass – and I had the experience recently of this – I went to Mass and I came to the Sign of Peace. There was someone there who couldn't give the Sign of Peace to one of our homeless residents who was at Mass with me. Yet that same person could still go down to receive the Eucharist. If Eucharist is a celebration of life (which is how I understand Eucharist) then we shouldn't be receiving Eucharist during one hour on a Sunday and then walking past the broken Body of Christ lying in the street.

Eucharist is about food and nourishment. Ludwig Feuerbach in *The Essence of Christianity* (1854) hit the nail on the head when he said that the problem with Christianity is that we make the real unreal and the unreal real. When we come to Eucharist we throw open the windows and drag this spiritual person through the door. We walk out and go past the hungry in the street. It's a mockery of Eucharist if we walk past the hungry. And we have the hungry here on our own doorstep. The hungry of Somalia, Mozambique, India: they are people who suffer in a very real way.

Feuerbach never got a teaching post because he was declared heretical. But I think many of his writings have become very relevant when we have a middle-class Church which shows feeble signs of benevolence towards the poor. If a social transformation has to come about, then it has to be those who suffer, themselves, *they* have to bring about that change, they have to mobilise themselves. I'm not calling for any kind of revolution, but I would speak against benevolence, the benevolence of the MP who spends an hour with the homeless under Blackfriars Bridge in London. I think that to find God we have to be at one with those who suffer.

The difference between Latin or Central America and Edinburgh is that when I was in Colombia I lived out in the country and there's a marked difference in poverty there. People in the country have arable land, they can at least have a garden to grow food. People in the city have virtually nothing, they have no land at all.

Perhaps one of the ironies about the Latin American city is the number of television aerials. I think you see the same thing here – the number of satellite dishes in deprived areas. I don't know whether it's just sheer boredom which leads people to run up huge debts to satellite TV companies. They pay the money for satellite movies, but don't have the money for food!

The difference in the poverty is that people here are very much like the untouchables of India, the *Dalits* to whom I'm very close. I've lived and worked with them.

I returned from India to Jericho House – suddenly my eyes opened and the Dalits were here in Edinburgh. They are people whom society has rejected and continues to reject, both at local government levels and in the Government's failure to fund vulnerable groups. I believe the community care legislation is a clear condemnation of people who are homeless or people with mental health problems.

The difficulty I have with Thatcherism is that it does not allow adequate resources to help fund vulnerable groups, believing society itself will help. But society has been so badly eroded by the enterprise culture.

I believe the role of the Church is to establish community. We are, after all, the People of God. There should be no distinction between clergy and laity (*laos* – Greek for 'people of God', 'called by God', 'convoked by God').

In essence God is standing alongside those who suffer. Those who suffer in Edinburgh and in British society suffer at the hands of the ruling powers, the dominant ideology (Thatcherism) and suffer also at the hands of the Church.

I remember somewhere reading a prayer:

*I was hungry and you went off to the chapel to
pray for me; I was thirsty and you gave me a
crucifix; I was homeless and you said 'God be
with you'. But I'm still hungry, thirsty and
homeless.*

God is not just in the Tabernacle. Prayer
is a very important element, but so is *action*.
The Church has to be involved at the grass-
roots level. Not just in benevolent handouts,
but in living and working with those who
suffer.

In Jericho House I see my role as not only
one of care for the homeless and solidarity
with the homeless, but also as a raising of
consciousness among the Christian churches
and at central and local government level.

I believe that transformation can come
about by all our homeless residents standing
up and being counted. By raising consciousness
among people who are powerless, change will
happen in their hearts.

LANTHORN

Revd James Maitland
Former CHURCH OF SCOTLAND MINISTER
Livingston

'Where is God?' Nieztsche's madman was asking that, going around with a lantern at midday, saying, 'Where is God?' He was looking for God, while all the people laughed at him and made a fool of him, saying, 'Has He gone away? Is He lost?' But he just kept on with his lantern: 'Where is God? Where is God?' A good, good question.

Our Ecumenical Experiment started as a result of two ecumenical conferences, one held at St Andrews in 1963, the other at Nottingham in 1965. Both of these conferences appealed to the church authorities in Scotland to try and do something different in Livingston (which had just been designated a new town); not to be content just to reproduce the old pattern of church life that we know so well in the new towns of Scotland.

Because of an initiative taken by our own presbytery here, through David Torrance, four churches agreed to designate the new town of Livingston an area of ecumenical experiment.

The Experiment was launched at Epiphany 1966. The Episcopal priest, Brian Hardy, and myself, a Church of Scotland minister, were inducted together, with Bishop and

Presbytery functioning together for the first time in recent Scottish history. That was done in the old Kirk of Calder at Midcalder.

The Roman Catholics had been approached quite informally by Bishop Ken Carey, the Episcopal bishop. He went to see Cardinal Gray asking if the Roman Catholics could be part of the Experiment. Cardinal Gray said no, the time was not ripe. So just these four on the Protestant side of the house came in.

In some ways the church buildings hindered, they queered the pitch for ecumenical development.

We'd been in here for perhaps three months – Brian Hardy, formerly chaplain at Downing College, Cambridge said, 'Right. The only way to work this is as a team'.

We went together to see Cardinal Gray and asked him to appoint a priest as soon as possible and to consider having Roman Catholic children go to the one school – the school where all the other children went. To the first request he was very sympathetic. He said, 'I've been thinking about this for a long time and have a priest in mind and I promise to have him on the ground before the end of the year'. And he was as good as his word. But he wouldn't discuss the school matter.

Father John Byrne came at the beginning of December 1966. He was with us for six or seven years. He suffered from cancer – but was a saint and had a tremendous Irish sense of humour and was a beautiful singer. On occasion he would even sing 'The Sash'! He was ideal. He had been chaplain for many years at Bangour Hospital and was well known and greatly loved. That really gave us a flying start.

Everything at the beginning happened at

the Riverside Primary School in Craigshill. There was that one building and the churches had their services there on Sunday and in between the services there was a free hour. We used that as a time when the people could meet and share their problems and difficulties. That came quite soon to be the New Town Forum. That really was what allowed life in the new town to get off the ground, because Roman Catholic people, Protestant people, church people, people with no church connections – all came together there, mixed and talked and worked together. That allowed a strong community life to develop very quickly.

Perhaps the early years could best be summed up in the words of Malcolm Drummond, our session clerk. After about two years we had a conference at Dunblane on the way in which church life was developing. Malcolm Drummond upset the theological pundits, including David Torrance, by saying, 'For us in Livingston, Church is the community; the community is the Church'. There is great truth in that.

At that time the Church of Scotland building – the first building to be put up – was St Columba's. Once that building went up, we, the Church of Scotland people, withdrew. And it wasn't just that church life became much thinner. It was community life that suffered. The Forum continued for a couple of years or longer, but was struggling all the time because we'd lost centre and focus.

I say all this because Lanthorn was born from all the struggles of these early years. Hamish Smith was the first Congregational minister. He was with us for four or five years before going as chaplain to Edinburgh University.

At that time the arrangement was that each denomination was responsible for putting up a building. The Church of Scotland put up St Columba's, the Episcopal Church put up St Paul's in Ladywell, and the Congregational Church was due to put up a church building over in Dedridge.

Hamish had the vision – this came out of our experience in Riverside and in our early years in Craigshill – to see that we wanted something different to allow church life and community life to enrich each other and not to be operating in the isolated way that churches tended to do.

He was very keen to take over some farm buildings there and use them as a church complex. But he moved to Edinburgh and Ross McLaren really did the most difficult thing of all – he took this vision of Hamish's and he gave it flesh and blood. He managed through his diplomacy and his administrative skills to bring together representatives of all the local authorities, and got them to agree to this shared centre, now called Lanthorn.

More than that, he got the Roman Catholic Church to agree. That we had never expected. Agreement was, and still is, to share a worship space in Lanthorn.

Livingston continues. The ecumenical commitment remains. The Ecumenical Experiment has become an Ecumenical Parish and I am so grateful to the Church of Scotland. We got hammered at the General Assembly, we got hammered into the ground – I've seen some of our ministers literally in tears over a speaker's disparagement. But the Assembly has always stood by us and said, 'Yes, you go forward'.

The Ecumenical Parish is now in existence

with five different congregations which are entitled to share full communion. It's the Lord's doing.

It was October 1968 when Bishop Carey gave permission for non-Episcopal ministers to officiate at Episcopal communions. That was a tremendous breakthrough.

There's a strong Covenanting influence and an Orange influence too in West Lothian; yet this has happened and it's happening nowhere else in Scotland. It's quite wonderful.

Alienation is a real problem in Livingston, yet what pleased us is the number of young people and children around here, and happily around here, relaxed, not stiff and formal and under duress.

The Lanthorn only covers Dedridge, but in a sense it expresses what Livingston is about – not just unity amongst church people, but unity throughout the life of the whole community.

This was the great experience of the early years. The community had so much to give to the Church. There was a real breaking down of barriers. The community was working.

We were grateful for the townplanning in that the landscaping was taken seriously and there was green all around. The origin of new towns in Britain was in the shattering experience the people of Britain had gone through at the time of the War when the evacuations from the cities took place and people were discovered living in impossible, degrading and dehumanising conditions.

It's difficult to recognise where you are in Livingston. Part of the difficulty is that this was to have been a new town where pedestrians were to be segregated from motor traffic. It is, to some extent, but it makes all sorts of problems – having folk walking in pedestrian routes that are often quiet, often dark, often dangerous.

We came up against the problems of young mothers. But if there's some liveliness and friendliness and good neigbourliness in a community, the old people have a place and are taken care of, without being pushed into separate clubs – and young mothers are part of things and don't feel lost.

As the town developed, Howden district came. People there felt there was nothing at all for them (and many young people still feel that); you've got many young mothers who had to go to the doctor and get tranquilising drugs. Livingston was described as 'Valium City'.

They put up a lot of flats in Craigshill that had a great many problems. Leaking homes – that was the first big issue that the Forum had to deal with. We came up against the Livingston Development Corporation because they said, 'Look, leave this alone, because we're attending to it'.

But the leaks went on and we felt we had to call in the MP. There was quite a show-down. But the result was that the Corporation did agree that they had to do something quite drastic. They took the people out of the flats and paid them compensation and brought them back after the repairs were completed.

I don't think this would ever have been done but for the presence of the Forum. All this come and go made for a real solidarity of life – for young mothers and older people and for children.

What we tried to develop was this close relationship between church and community.

That became much more difficult once we had a separate building. But we had a system of visitors in every street in Craigshill.

Then Norman McCallum, a young Episcopal priest from Ballachulish, was appointed. He had had training in sociology and experience in social work. He took up this whole way of being in touch with the community and allowing the community to feel that the church was here for them and was open to them, and was in some sense a servant to the people and to the community.

The Forum was open to everyone in Craigshill and dealt with every issue people wanted to bring up. Malcolm Drummond, the session clerk, was also landscaping and forestry officer and he would make grain available for sowing grass. For the other more serious matters, we had to work on the authorities!

All over the world the churches are being made new by being made *local*. I would say we have a long way to go in Livingston to let the unity of God's People take on greater meaning and become a much more exciting reality. But it's there and it's slowly developing.

What becomes clearer and clearer is that the whole Gospel's about the kind of things Livingston's struggling with. Jesus at his last journey to Jerusalem brings his ministry to a climax in the Palm Sunday entrance – the King riding on an ass. He comes in to the town claiming to be King and cleanses the Temple and spends at least two days teaching all-comers in the Temple.

According to Matthew, Jesus' last word to the people (as distinct from his speaking to the disciples) was 'O, Jerusalem, Jerusalem, how often would I have gathered your children together as a hen gathers her brood under her wings, and you would not let me'.

Then he says, 'Where is your Temple? Deserted of God'. As God's prophet and God's Son, Jesus is saying that when we cease to want to be together as the Children of God, sharing some kind of family life, then we may have all the trappings – (and they had it all in the Temple: sacrifices, prayers and psalms and the festival) – but we will be deserted, desolate of the Spirit.

Jesus raised the new Temple through the Cross; and the Resurrection was His Body, this new community of all God's children.

We have a real chance in Livingston to give some embodiment to this.

ACADEMIC COMMUNITY

Father Gilbert Marcus
Former DOMINICAN
(ROMAN CATHOLIC) CHAPLAIN
University of Edinburgh

God is everywhere. There's no particular place where God is more than anywhere else. But that's not implicit in calling a place a 'holy place'. It doesn't say there's anything special about the place which is to do with God being there more than anywhere else. It's to do with human history – that men and women mediate God to each other through the way they pray together, preach the Gospel to each other, show each other mercy, feed the hungry – the whole Christian community's life-patterns. And we're not just abstract, bodiless beings, 'talking heads'.

We live in a history, we live in a society, we live in places. So certain places have meaning for us, not because God is more present there, but because the history of those *places* – and the history of a community with respect to those places – is more meaningful and we are different when we are in those places.

The places are the same. God is the same – He's universally present. But we are different by virtue of our relationships with each other in different places. We're spatial beings, we live in architecture, we live in geography, we live in road-maps.

And so holy places are to do with relationships of a community and the memory of a community of what has happened in certain places: the place where the first preacher of the Gospel landed in a country – Whithorn, in Scotland, for example, where Ninian appeared. Places where people who are of importance for our community tradition were born or died or were buried. It's not to do with anything special in the place. It's to do with a community's symbolic articulation of its identity and its purpose.

If there is a Christian witness in this community – in this case, it's the students and staff of the University of Edinburgh – they're my parishioners, as it were.

If we can create a community where people hear the Gospel, celebrate the sacraments, share in the vision of the Kingdom of God which Jesus offers us; if people show mercy in a community; if they find companionship or material support when they're poor and emotional support when they're depressed, then people will find God here. God is not an additional extra on top of all the other things that we offer.

God is what is offered when you offer mercy, God is what is offered when you offer the vision of the Kingdom of God. That is what it means for God to be present. It's not an additional factor along with all the other things.

God is in no way dependent on us, but we're dependent on Him. He has shown us there are certain ways of human behaviour which will reveal the presence of God to people and which will actualise God's presence in their lives – through preaching, through sacraments, through this community life, through the witness of the Church.

People don't just grow up believing that God forgives them. They have to be told that God is merciful. And if you show them mercy and articulate that mercy through the sacraments, through your relationships with people and through the creation of a merciful community where people don't judge each other but accept each other, then people will begin to understand the mercy of God.

As in all places, there's an absence of community in Edinburgh. Old people who feel unwanted; poor people who feel rejected and useless, unemployed and unvalued; homeless people; junkies; people with AIDS. Better-off people who also feel unloved. Like any town, any city. How do we reach out to them, how do we make those people feel valued? It's a constant challenge to the whole Church and sometimes we're very good at it and sometimes we fail completely.

One of my students worked in the Camera Obscura and all the tourists used to appear. You look around the city and the guide on the Camera Obscura highlights certain parts of the city which you can see from the tower. Normally it was things like the High Kirk and the touristy places. But the student would point out a little primary school in one of the deprived areas of the city where three-quarters of the parents were unemployed, and he would talk to the tourists about the social reality of people who've become truly invisible in the city. One of the things about poverty is that it makes you invisible. Your problems, your pain, aren't important to people who've got money and resources. And I think part of the job of the Church is to give a voice to those people who have no voice and to make visible those people who are invisible.

Part of the prophecy of Isaiah about 'opening the eyes of the blind' is actually about helping people to see the reality of the world which we've created. Not just to see the misery, but to see the beauty as well. And also to see the hope, to see the possibilities we have for changing things. People may very well see the sufferings and the problems but be blind to the possibilities of change – just not have hope and be unable to see an alternative vision. They feel 'we're impotent and we can't do anything; this is the way things are, this is the way things have to be'. Part of the Gospel is that it doesn't have to be this way. Sometimes that's seen as a promise, sometimes it's seen as a threat. This is the God 'who casts the mighty from their thrones and lifts up the lowly, who fills the hungry with good things and sends the rich away empty'.

That overturning of the orders of injustice is an important part of the Gospel. It can sound threatening to people.

MUSLIM

Imam Abdelhafid Selougha
The Central Mosque, Edinburgh

God, by nature, is a unique deity. Whether in physical or other terms, he is supreme. He has no beginning and no end. He has nothing in common with human beings.

But God created man to know him by instinct. Man will not be able to define God, but he knows that there must be a supreme power – a superpower.

God is above everything else. If you want to love people, the best way is through God himself – loving a person for his own actions in accordance with what God has revealed. You only hate a person when he is disobeying God.

God is everywhere – whether you are in the heart of the earth or outside in the heavens.

God can only be known through real revelation which comes from messengers and prophets. But God is greater than revelation – he is the revealer. And there are different ways in which he reveals – either directly (through prophets) or indirectly through angels.

God cannot be described. Nothing is equal to God, or similar to him. You cannot even try to make his shape. But he will reveal himself. Yet only to the true believers.

He spoke to Moses directly, without any intermediary. Moses tried to know God ('O

God, allow me to see you') but failed. God told him he wouldn't be able to see him. Moses pleaded, 'Just allow me a glimpse of you'. So God said, 'Look at that mountain. If you can see the mountain, then you can see me'. Then the mountain shattered and Moses fell down unconscious and did not wake up until quite some time had passed.

We do believe that all the messengers and prophets were sent by God – by Allah (meaning 'the only Being that should be worshipped with complete and absolute devotion').

There is no difference whatsoever between the revelations of each prophet, except in terms of life or legislation. God develops his legislation in line with the mental development of human beings.

God is truly present. He is the only being that was not created. He wouldn't be God if he had an end or a beginning. The best way to experience God is to worship him and obey his commands.

Yet nobody is at the level of being completely obedient to God. We all fail from time to time. That's exactly the meaning of Creation – nothing is perfect except God. That's how he created us. Otherwise we'd be the opposite of him or equal to him.

Nothing and nobody is perfect, we all make mistakes. But that's the sweetness of worshipping him. We sometimes disobey him, then we repent.

Everything has been created by God but nothing is imposed on people by God. People commit crimes and do evil according to their own choice.

There are rules in Nature – if you touch fire, it hurts you, burns you. That's a law created by God. So keep away from fire. Anything that happens (even if you choose to do it yourself on purpose) is destiny. Destiny is known to God. If it will happen, it will happen – you cannot escape it.

This doesn't mean that God deliberately puts you in this situation. He tests people. But testing people doesn't necessarily mean that he punishes them. In fact God only tests those he loves.

He knows your faith. If God tests you, it means he loves you. He never tests you as far as to destroy your faith. He tests you in order to allow you to know your own faith.

After death all people enter an intermediate stage until every human being dies. Then there will be the Hereafter and the Judgement of people for their misconduct in life.

A person is only punished according to what he knows. Human beings all share a minimum amount of knowledge – for example, to know that there must be a God and that there is a God who should be worshipped.

But if you know that there is a God and he should be worshipped and you did it in your own way and you've never heard of *Islam* ('submission to God'), you will be judged only in accordance with your faith, not for your actions.

NUNRAW

Right Revd Donald McGlynn
ABBOT OF NUNRAW
Sancta Maria Abbey,
Nunraw, East Lothian

Tucked away on a plateau above the village of
Garvald, East Lothian, is Nunraw, home of
the Cistercian monks.

Abbot Donald explained that the building
of the new monastery began in 1952 and
ended in 1969: 'They were building when we
moved in. During the summer holidays we
had the workers' camp – builders and students,
coming to help with the labouring. For
something like 20 years we worked at the
construction. Now all the central community
locations – the refectory, scriptorium, library
and dormitory are completed. We use the
scriptorium as a community room for meetings and as a library. We've used one wing to
improvise a space for the present Abbey
church (we haven't built the real church yet –
that'll come some day). We haven't built the
guesthouse either because the old Nunraw
House serves that purpose.

'The old house is used as a retreat-house.
It can take up to 60 people, but as we're
short-staffed we try to make the limit about
30. It's for resident guests. There's no limit
on day-guests or coach-parties. We still get
parish outings on a Sunday – but on nothing

like the scale of days gone by.'

Being a Cistercian monk involves manual labour: in Nunraw's case, farming.

'Our farm is 500 hectares,' added Abbot Donald, 'for the fattening of cattle. It's all been simplified. When I first came there were beef cattle, sheep, a dairy, potatoes, pigs, poultry.

'When I became Abbot around 1970, numbers had diminished, the Nunraw community was getting older. We had to rationalise. So gradually we shed a lot of the lesser departments and concentrated on the beef herd, rearing calves for the market.

'We're self-sufficient only so far as the beef-fattening unit is able to finance the monastery. Another thriving department was the garden, a big walled garden. But we haven't got the manpower any more to work it. Today it's a question of buying whatever we need from the market.

'The effect we've had on the people around the Abbey has been that of a friendly centre, creating a good-neighbourly atmosphere. We've the best of relations with Garvald village close by.

'When the monks first came in 1946 there were few Roman Catholics in Garvald. The villagers were warned about the terrible monks. When the monks came, many of the villagers had all their doors shut and curtains drawn. They were frightened.

'That following Spring there was a snow storm, the first for decades. The village was blocked off and snowed in for about six weeks. This meant supplies were short. But the monks had milk from the dairy herd and they had made bread. So they took milk and bread down to the village for the children. From that day forward it has never been forgotten and we're the greatest of friends.

'The ground plan of this monastery is the same as that of Melrose, Newbattle, Dundrennan and Sweetheart. Sometimes the monks shifted the foundations slightly to accommodate a local river which was used for driving a mill, for the water-supply to the ablutions block, for the cookhouse. It usually flowed under the kitchen. Sometimes they even had a fish-pond.'

Unhappily, the community at Nunraw has declined in numbers over the years. 'There are 20 monks here at present,' Abbot Donald admitted, facing reality in the face. 'In the 1960s the laybrothers were incorporated with the monks. Now we're all primarily monks and some also happen to be priests.'

Things are not, however, as bad as they might seem. The Abbot has cause for confidence: 'The international Orders such as ourselves have got an advantage over smaller Orders. Vocations in Western Europe are very few in number. Looking at it from a UK point of view, things at the moment are pretty dismal. But worldwide, the Order is as healthy as ever. It's just a matter of waiting for the turn of the tide. We're at low-ebb now, but the low-ebb gives as much glory to the Lord as the full tide.'

The cloisters at Nunraw were built with voluntary labour. Much of the material was second-hand. The plate-glass windows in the cloisters came from the demolition of big stores in Glasgow and Edinburgh. The marble steps came from Galbraith's in Paisley.

The outside stonework of the Abbey is random-pattern built with volcanic 'rattle-bag' stone from nearby Dirleton.

The monastery is not without decoration. A fine piece of sculpture on the refectory wall was roughed-out with a pneumatic drill by a Miss Henderson, a member of the Church of Scotland.

'The monks eat a vegetarian diet,' points out the Abbot. 'It's not an ideological matter, but a question of poverty and simplicity of life. St Benedict's idea was that monks shouldn't eat the flesh of four-footed animals, but he seems to have allowed fish and chickens.

'In every monastery you would have had provision for guests. The community here has a table in the refectory for the Infirmary, for the aged and sick. On feastdays we have fish. Each place is set with a napkin, a plate, a cup and a jug of water. Most of the kitchen was equipped from scrap-yards.'

At one end of the refectory is a raised dais like a disc-jockey's with a lectern and a micro-phone. 'We always have reading at lunchtime. We start off with the Bible and then have some topical book.'

The week's duties are pinned up above the reader's desk: leading the Office, serving in the Church, serving the lunch, washing-up. 'Our services are all in English now,' explained the Abbot, 'except for the *Salve Regina*.'

The book bindery no longer functions: 'Now that we have the technology to print choir-books ourselves, we reproduce the large letters with a computer,' said Abbot Donald. Today he has swapped his tractor for a computer with desk-top publishing software, a scanner and laser-printer.

What are monasteries for? Abbot Donald is quite clear on that point: 'The church living the life of the Church. There isn't anyone else praying the seven hours of the Divine Office.

The Community represents the body of the faithful. We're going back to the first Christian community in the Acts of the Apostles. A monastery is a Christian family writ large.

'When I came there wasn't a tree here. But just before he died, Abbot Columba Mulcahy planted shrubs and trees. When we had a large Marian Year pilgrimage here four or five years ago, the altar in the enclosure was sheltered under the tall screen of the trees.'

Life for the monks is not a bed of roses. Their daily routine would put off most urban 'couch-potatoes'.

'We get up at 3.15 am and begin with the vigils followed by meditation for half an hour, then the community Mass at 4.45 and at 5.30 a light breakfast. Bedtime is around 8.00 pm,' said the Abbot. 'One of the reasons for getting up so early in the morning is because at that time the human mind is truly open and receptive. It's the best time to pray.'

Nunraw is the latest in a long line of Cistercian communities in Scotland. The Cistercians were heavily involved in the surrounding areas. They introduced many new agricultural methods. They had big farms – Newbattle, for example, extended right across Scotland to Monklands. They were great sheep-farmers, managing a large economy, although they themselves were an enclosed community.

King David I had founded the abbeys not only out of piety but, in the Borders, as a protection against the English and to extend his own political influence. The monks employed lay people in their industries. Every monastery had its Infirmary. The monasteries were the nearest thing to a National Health Service.

Down at the old Nunraw House with its red sandstone walls, Father Raymond is in charge of the guesthouse. 'It's only possible to run this popular facility for the general public because the guests themselves do the washing-up and contribute what they can financially.'

Marlene Welsh from Glasgow was having lunch. She commented, 'We've been coming here for twelve years. We're here for seven days. It's a very special place. It's a place where you can have a week right out from the world, away from the TV, wireless, papers, the shops, the family pressures; to be peaceful, to deepen your spirituality.

'You can sit down, as I did this morning for about an hour, talking to one of the monks. He's a very wise person. He's been here for a long time. I ask him things about my faith that I don't understand. He can give the answers that you're looking for. If you have any kind of problems, they're the people to put you on the right road.

'You also meet people from all walks of life. Something always draws you back. You come here for the *spirituality.* I think God brings you here for a reason.

'People become monks not because it's an easy life – it's as hard as being married. They're still having to live in community and cope with the irritations of their companions just like a marriage. It's not a running away from the world.

'They're still in the world and they're coping with the same pressures as we are.'

THE
SAMARITANS

Betty
Befriender to People in Crisis

As far as we're concerned, our title has no
religious connotation at all, although we were
founded in London by an Anglican priest and
journalist, Chad Varah. He worked at the
time in St Stephen's, Wandsworth in the City
of London, in the Square Mile.

At that time there were two suicides a day
in London and he felt it was high time something was done about it.

He called people together and advertised
the fact that he would be in the crypt of a
local church to help people.

Chad Varah had many friends in the newspaper world. When he thought of starting
this organisation he got in touch with his
newspaper friends and told them what he
planned to do. And it was his newspaper
contacts who gave us our title. They wrote:
'Come and tell your problems to the Samaritan
priest.' Chad Varah thought it was a good
name for his new organisation, but, that
aside, we have no religious affiliation at all.

What we do is along broadly similar lines
to the work of the churches. But there are
people who would never contact a church. A
lot of our people probably have strong church
connections, but they choose to come to us.

It's a 24-hour phone line but our premises

are open for callers from nine in the morning to half past nine at night. We don't have an appointment system – you can just pop in. We have 27,000 contacts a year – phones and visitors. Between four and five per cent of our contacts are visitors.

People, when they've got problems like that, don't want to go to somebody who knows them. The last people they'll speak to is their own families. They sometimes wouldn't want to speak to their doctor and certainly wouldn't want to speak to their minister or to their priest.

They want someone who's standing back, who doesn't know them at all. It's the anonymity that they like. We guarantee that.

I often say to people, 'What can I call you?' Judging by the 'Johns' and 'Marys' and the 'Annes' that we have, you don't always get the right name from them. That doesn't matter.

I feel very sad when I hear stories about people and I think, 'You can't imagine that going on in that sort of household'. People have got so much materially and yet have so little at the end of the day. They don't have a happy family life and yet they have the where-withall (you'd think) to have it. That saddens me.

I would say more women phone us than men. In Scotland more men commit suicide than women by a ratio of three to one, but the female suicide rate has gone up.

Probably they think that's the only thing to do – to kill themselves. We are not here to tell people not to kill themselves. I've got no right to tell you whether you should take your own life or not. We're here just to listen to people, to let them sort out their feelings. At the end of the day they could well go away, put the phone down and kill themselves. On the other hand, maybe by talking to us they may see a light at the end of the tunnel and decide, 'Well, maybe it's not such a good thing to do after all. Life is sweet; let's give it another go'.

This is what we insist that people understand – that we're not going to persuade them not to take their own lives. That is something that our volunteers, when they come first, find difficult to come to terms with. Your natural instinct is to stop a person from doing that. We never give advice; so you can't tell them what to do. You can just listen to them and hope that by talking it through, they may see a way out of their problems.

Poverty is a big problem. We have a lot of people with money difficulties. A lot of homelessness is due to financial problems. Unemployment. You name it and we get it here.

It's a very privileged position to be the only one standing between a person and death. It takes a lot of courage.

Our clients may well believe in God but they may well also wonder where He's gone when they're in the depths. They could well feel rejected and let down – as we all do at times.

If they're all right and things are going right, life in Edinburgh's great. But if they're down ….

It's amazing how many people come from outside to Edinburgh, thinking that they're going to make it here. And then they get a 'dropper', to put it bluntly. They come up here and say, 'Look, we've come from _____ to Edinburgh. It's not working out. What should I do?'

Edinburgh at night can be a bit rough. The people who work here at night can tell you about the noise and the fracas.

Having lived in London for 21 years I was very surprised when I came back to Edinburgh to find that there's all this unhappiness, violence (domestic violence), the drug scene – all the things you didn't expect in this very respectable city.

On the surface it's a very respectable place, but working as we do here – we know only too well there's such a lot goes on.

We're listening to all classes of people. This is one of the things which hits you about domestic violence – it's not the man coming in from his work with his pay packet on a Friday night, having spent most of it in the pub on the way home; it's members of the legal profession, of the medical profession, 'professional' people. Abuse goes across the board, it's not confined to one (I hate the word) 'class' of people.

We get a lot of teenagers calling us – the typical teenager doesn't get on with his (or her) parents. Then parents call us up to say they can't get on with their teenagers.

We have people who have been with us for a long time. We are basically a crisis organisation, so we don't really like to encourage dependency. We like to help people over a hump, as it were, and then wean them away from us. That, originally, is what we were founded for.

But, with the best will in the world, they do keep on coming back and there's not a lot we can do about it.

When I started here in the 1970s we used to have a lot of men who came in. We had a supply of disposable razors and paper towels and they used to come in for a wash and brush-up on a Sunday morning. That has more or less stopped now.

We still have those who come in and present you with a mini-problem and then say, 'Can I have a cup of tea, please? Make a pot, not just a cup'. Which makes you think that what they're after is just that – a wee bit of companionship, a cup of tea and a biscuit.

ECUMENICAL
COMMUNITY

Father Roland Walls
Houses of the Transfiguration

Not far from the ornate Roslin Chapel in
Midlothian (with its historic Prentice Pillar)
stands a weatherbeaten green tin shack, a
former Miners Institute saved from demolition
in 1965 only by a last-minute donation from
a local benefactor.

In glorious sunshine the mischievous
cherubic smile of Father Roland welcomes the
visitor. He leans on the wooden gate, drawing
meditatively on his pipe. Behind him on the
gable-end of the Houses of the Transfiguration
(founded to promote Christian unity) hangs a
sign in Gaelic *'Comaraich'* (sanctuary) below a
gnarled wish-bone branch of an ancient tree
from a bog in Sutherland. This is his
'Bhuddist garden' ('the Lord is the gardener').
He points out an even more twisted antique
root, shaped like a man. 'That's what we call
the Devil,' smiles Father Roland. 'He's fleeing
– I hope!'

Inside the communal house, coffee is on the
boil. Here is not only a community which is
ecumenical and open to all, but one which is
able to reaffirm the value of the discarded and
the decayed, an oasis of reality in a world of
polystyrene, without telephone or television.

Brother John, an Anglican priest and Prior of the house, works as a labourer stripping down cars for re-painting. Father Roland, an Anglican priest for over 40 years, was ordained a Roman Catholic priest in 1983. He has the gift of prising people open with the challenge of his humour and insight. His community of three, basing their lives on the rules of Benedict ('sobriety') and Francis ('that's where the wildness comes in!') have their cells and their chapel in the back garden of the house where silence is maintained at all times. Their cells, garden sheds of treated wood and roofs of black felt, most of us would find constricting; their mattresses are stout wooden doors. In the chapel with its 'feminist icon' showing the valuable role of women in the church, was the most telling example of the Community's cherishing of the ordinary things in life – Stations of the Cross made from two used matchsticks pierced by a pin. The over-whelming impression of Father Roland and the Houses of the Transfiguration was of a Community at the leading edge of religious life.

'If he's the God of the Bible,' said Father Roland, 'God is interested in the pluralism of love. Love not only endures but rejoices in diversity – as in the Blessed Trinity itself. I'm more and more inclined to go back to avoiding the word "God" as often as possible because I notice in the Fathers of the Church – the early Greek Fathers and the Latin Fathers – they like to call God by his proper name of "Father, Son and Holy Spirit" (or the *Trias* – Trinity).

'We've got to get into the habit of doing this because it immediately points out what He's up to. It's the Trinity of a love-relationship whose essence and unity is love in a diversification of persons. So it gives some clue as to what He does and what He is. As I've lived here for 30 years, I believe that one of the attractive sides of Midlothian is that, unlike some other rather touristic counties, Midlothian contains this extraordinary diversity. But it also has its struggles towards unity which is always fraught and always has to be remade again and again (rather like love-affairs anywhere).

'I'm interested in the county-God and this particular effort of trying to get people to, not just tolerate diversity, but rejoice in it. It is a stage of maturity in the human person that he or she can do this.

'Normally speaking, our adolescence includes a certain intolerance. You bolt yourself down into a certain class or educational or economic background. You find yourself a comfortable nest in whatever you've been born into and fall into the routine of getting it going.

'Whereas the world at large, in this county in particular – its future and its happiness and its viability is going to depend on whether we've got enough people working away to change what persons in society look like.

'It's only when we're persons in society, in community, that we're going to reflect as the Bible says 'the image of the God who made us'. It's only thus that we're going to understand what he's up to (and always has been up to).

'It is very important, it seems to me, that we localise very particularly and rejoice when people are going to write or speak or work for a particular "locality". I'm very optimistic about the present situation because in this sort of homelessness, exile and alienation (that have been going on at least from the Industrial Revolution) there's been a reaction in the past twenty years: people speaking on the media and writing about "locality" and "characters" have become very popular. Such books and programmes have a good commercial selling-value which indicates to me that there's a need for roots and a seeking for roots.

'In my own life, I was born into a very rooted family in the Isle of Wight and for the first part of my life I wandered from work in Leeds, Sheffield and Cambridge. Then I found myself up in Midlothian in a broken-down mining village. I've lived now 30 years here and my need for roots isn't to return to my original soil in the Isle of Wight. I've found myself joining little families and in the things that go on in a Midlothian village and finding my rootedness in this.

'If anyone asks me what I've been thankful for, it is that I found myself in such a place. It's very important that people should be affirmed not only in their jobs and their activities, but in their locality. It's to do with faith.

'"Home" is one of the most powerful words you can use in a sermon. However dreary you are in a sermon, if you use the word "Home" you get attention for that sentence.

'This homelessness (for lots of people, a will-o'-the-wisp image at the back of their minds – something that corresponds to the open fire and the slippers), I think can be healed in a locality. That locality is the place where you can think about a God who is Home because He's love, who is love because He's diversity in unity. Wherever these two words "God" and "Home" appear (whether in economics, social developments, family problems or successes, in the Church and in the Church's unity and disunity) they are of paramount importance.

'If you want a laboratory where you can look at these words in detail, then this county is as good as any in Britain.'

EXILE

Ziegfried Sapietis, *SCULPTOR*
Newbattle Cottage

Tall, bearded and wearing glasses, Ziegfried
Sapietis lives in a cottage facing Newbattle
Abbey in Dalkeith. You step off the busy
main road into another world – a workshop
cluttered with works of art, all shapes and
sizes, mostly of wood and covered with a thick
layer of dust, the product of the carving and
grinding which is the daily life of the sculptor.

Mr Sapietis is a Latvian who dreams of the
forests of his country and the log cabin where
he grew up, where he was able to cycle for
miles between the trees. One wall of his workshop is stacked with 17 wooden boards (three
more await completion) on which the tragic
story of his people and his own life is gouged.

'This is my *Chronicle*, the other side of the
coin,' he explains. 'I fought for the Latvian
National Resistance and was in a German
prison and concentration camp in Latvia under
the Gestapo. Then I fought in the Latvian
Legion against the Russians. I was wounded
and sent to Germany. From Sunemunde in
Germany, with my leg in plaster, I escaped in
1945 to Denmark.'

THE CHRONICLE

It starts with empire-builders from all races, as

you can see from the flags and the ship that transported millions of men and women who were sold into slavery.

Then comes Stalin and his deportation camps. It began in 1917 when Lenin became ruler of the Red Empire. He killed and burned the Tsar and his family, turned churches into stables and cinemas. He forbade the worship of God and established one-party rule and secret police terror. He promised the workers that they would have Paradise.

In 1924 Lenin died and was proclaimed a saint, embalmed and placed in a marble mausoleum to be worshipped by friends and enemies.

Stalin was then worshipped and heralded as son, teacher and father. He became the greatest murderer in history. He killed, tortured and starved to death 30 million people. He deported into slave-camps, imprisoned and worked to death another 30 million.

In 1940 Stalin's armies and tanks invaded the Baltic countries and occupied them for 50 years. One tenth of the population escaped into exile, one tenth was deported for work in prison camps, many thousands were executed and imprisoned. Finally the Red invaders outnumbered the native population.

Forgotten were countless bodies of slave labourers (buried or not buried) scattered over the endless Arctic tundra of Russia.

In 1991 in the Baltic countries the underbelly of the Red octopus was punctured by the broken bones of its crushed victims and the Communist empire ended. But mass graves with battered heads and skulls marked the invaders' road from the Baltic to the Polar regions.

'I've lived in this house since I finished my studies. I'm very grateful to the Scots because they gave me a chance and scholarships, so I shall never forget it.

'I was a country boy but I lived for some time in Riga.

'This place has meant a lot to me. I bought this one acre and its deserted, condemned cottages in 1960. I renovated them and planted three hundred trees.

'Where my studio is, the building is about three hundred years old. The adjoining two-storey is two hundred years old. The house stands on what used to be the Great London Road and in my garden are the remains of Newbattle village, only foundations left. Beside my house is what used to be the old Sun Inn. Across the road is Newbattle Abbey, former home of the Marquess of Lothian.

'I worked for four years on my house. The roofs were torn down and rebuilt. All the old plasterboarding was taken out from the walls and replaced, new floors were put in.

'I feel very deeply for every suppressed nation in the world. Once you start suppressing other people you're not nationalist but imperialist or chauvinist. I feel that empire-builders have suppressed many people and killed millions and caused much suffering.

'In my country we had vast numbers of trees. Here I try to plant as many trees as I can.

'I'm a Lutheran Protestant. I believe in God but I'm a freethinker. I don't believe anybody can give me a formula.

'Recently I advertised and found one friend from Latvia (who died not long after). We were in prison together in Riga. Another friend who was with me in prison and concentration camp is a professor of architecture in Riga. Another is in the USA.

'In spite of everything I'm a hopeful

person. I'm an optimist. I believe in struggle. But I don't want people to forget the lessons of the past. My next project is a Statement of Crosses – concentration-camp crosses about three metres high.

'I lived in Denmark for some years before I came to Scotland. I studied at the Royal Academy in Copenhagen where I got my Design foundation. Then in 1960 I spent my travelling scholarship from Edinburgh College of Art studying in Italy, Sweden and Denmark. The Danes are fine craftsmen. They don't believe in falsifying materials: brick is brick and stone is stone.

'I work mainly in wood for the simple reason that I come from a country where there were a lot of forests and I grew up surrounded by trees. My father had a little farm and there were forests where you could cycle for six miles seeing maybe an occasional forester's cottage. I also like stone and clay: these are my main media. To me sculpture is the art of three-dimensional form. Carving is the most expressive of the arts. When you create a work of art you express some feeling in a language where there are rules and limits.'

Ziegfried Sapietis points to two large wooden figures of a man and a woman locked in an embrace.

'In sculpture there has to be some deeper experience behind the work. That sculpture is based on old chimneys left in a Latvian town which I saw in a magazine. Everybody needs bread and butter and potatoes. Everybody might need a plumber. But you have to accept that there is only a small minority who feel that they have a real need for any kind of art. As an artist I don't work for anybody, I just work for myself.'

HIGH STREET
WORSHIP

Revd Gilleasbuig Macmillan
CHURCH OF SCOTLAND MINISTER
St Giles Kirk, High Street, Edinburgh

I'm not sure how useful a word the word
'God' is. There certainly was one theologian
– I think, Paul Tillich – who said that he
thought it had been so misunderstood and
misapplied that it would be healthy and
probably necessary for it to be out of use for
about two or three hundred years before it
could be captured and re-discovered. I think
there's something in that.

From a Christian point of view (*any*
Christian point of view), the person of Jesus as
the focus of worship is what I mean by 'GOD'.

I can't think of a big father-figure in the
sky. So what is this worship which I am
focusing on the personality and character of
Jesus?

It is an attempt to detect a certain wholeness in life – that we are part of something
large; that somehow the whole universe can
be conceived as a unity.

The American educational philosopher,
John Dewey, round about 1930, said that he
had come to the conclusion that the word
'GOD' meant nothing more and nothing less
than the *sense of self* being able to identify
itself with the universe as a whole.

That's not orthodox Christianity, but

equally, it's not as thin as it sounds. There's something very deep and profound about that. It is the sense that life has a wholeness.

Worship is an orientation of oneself (not necessarily to the East!) – it is a re-directing of oneself. It's a putting oneself in a context where one sees that one's not at the centre of things, that one's part of a very large whole that applies to the balance of feelings within oneself. We often overdo our intellect or certain aspects of ourselves. The purpose of a ritual act performed regularly is bringing-together.

Buildings can do that for us, sometimes better than the events which happen in them. I think of the wonderful television programme that John Betjeman did 20 or 30 years ago, in which he visited the churches in the county of Norfolk.

There was one parish church he visited on a week-day. Betjeman was standing at the door of the church wearing a boater, a plastic mac, holding a cane, with a little Jack Russell dog at the end of a lead.

'The Rector is saying evensong, the villagers are not here. The villagers are never here on a week-day, but they know that the Rector's doing it. And that's what matters.'

People who count the success or failure of Christianity by numbers or by money would laugh at that. But there's something important in that sense of vicarious worship. Church buildings and worship going on (whether or not you're doing it yourself), represent a reminder of the holy and of the unity of life and that the personality and character and standards of Jesus are our way of saying what that importance is and how it's best responded to.

So I'm not ready to make a distinction between pilgrims and tourists. I'm not ready to make a distinction between God and the wholeness of life. I'm not ready to make a distinction between what happens on Sunday mornings and what happens on Thursday afternoons.

I do think that such services are terribly important and I'm very keen that anyone who comes to a church service here should not see something that's schismatic or sectarian; that they should have a vision of the richest sense of catholic Christianity. By 'catholic' I don't just mean Western – we've an awful lot to learn from the Orthodox tradition. Nowadays we've got to learn from the new Church, the Church in Latin America and other places in the Third World.

I would like people who come here (from any Christian background) to find things that are familiar and to find things that are stimulating and different – whether they come from the Church of Scotland parish along the street, from Roman Catholic Spain or Baptist Alabama or Pentecostalist Brazil. That's what church worship should do for anybody anywhere. There should be a sense of the wide catholicity of the whole Christian world. There should also be a sense of things that take you by surprise and catch your breath afresh on a Sunday.

There are many people who take the view that the Church must represent standards different from those of the community; must be challenging the state, the local authority, the public at large; and must attempt to do things in a Christian way (which the secular arm can't do).

I think that I won't give up Christendom

without a struggle. The idea of people not knowing the names of their physical neighbours as they rush off in their cars to engage in Christian fellowship with their ecclesiastical comrades, leaves me somewhat uncomfortable. I would prefer they didn't know the people they worshipped with and found the worship stimulating, but knew the people they actually lived near.

Worship should be related to the real and natural community of physical proximity. Worship should not create an artificial club or recreational community around churches. What the community does for the better disposition of its resources in the ups and downs of attempting to help people and trying to create a just and fair society, will have influence which comes from people who hide behind pillars in churches. Hymns, prayers and readings can move them and provoke them to do things on a Monday – to write to their MP (or perhaps they may *be* MPs!), which nobody knows was the result of a Christian or church influence. There will be others who do the same sort of thing and who knows what their impetus was?

I've been here at St Giles for 20 years and in that time I've baptised only four children living within my own territorial parish. That must be about the smallest number in Scotland of any parish minister.

I've baptised children living in the Middle East, in the south of England, in America and in all sorts of other parts of Edinburgh, but very few in this area.

Houses are being rehabilitated in the High Street, and that's very nice, but very often they're not families. They're young people, young couples and older people. There are even fewer local shops than when I first came. There are more tourist shops, but fewer places where you can buy bread and groceries.

Fashions go up and down. We inhabit the cultural climate of our time. It's quite difficult to go against it. The Lowland Scot, for centuries, has rarely been a person of noted public mysticism (I speak as a Highlander!), but then Lowlands and Highland and Irish have mixed a great deal in the last 150 years, so that there's a fair amount of stirring of that genetic pot.

I certainly think I mix with a fairly wide cross-section of the community in one way or another, and I would have thought that the sort of impulses, the sense of transcendence, the sense of mystery, the sense of a need and wish for some sort of all-embracing unity in life (and a wish to be attached to traditional Christianity in some degree) – these things are there. The fashions and habits of allegiance to churches go up and go down.

If one were to measure church attendance today and compare it with church attendance a hundred years ago, I imagine you would find that (in certain sections of the community at any rate) there was a higher proportion attending churches then.

If you were to compare it with attendance two hundred years ago, you might well come to the opposite conclusion. Round about the end of the eighteenth century, a lot of people started writing pamphlets about the decline of Christianity – Christian morals were going to the wall, hardly anybody was attending public worship. These things go up and down.

One of the biggest differences today is that, in the past, there was a sort of prevailing assumption that Christianity was the orthodoxy from which you deviated (even if ninety per cent of the people were deviating at a time, that was still the official religion).

That is not so among many people today. There's much more of a sense of acceptance of diversity and of pluralist culture. There is, perhaps, a rumour of the Church being in decline, which perhaps did not to the same extent accompany the previous periods of trough and dip. Perhaps these rumours – the interpretations of identical facts – can make the facts behave quite differently in their impact?

The Church has survived tremendous poverty in the past from industrial squalor and also dreadful conditions in the Highlands. People were too poor to have time for church. There was an investigation of life in the Highlands a hundred and fifty years ago. A lot of people said: 'We don't have clothes to go to church.' The church was often too far away, anyway. The idea of this church-going Scottish past is not as clear and straightforward a notion as people imagine.

Edinburgh has both the benefit and the draw-back of being a bureaucratic city, a city of pen-pushers, or of people who used to push pens and who now push word-processors.

QUAKERS

Mr Alan Longman
CONVENER OF THE ELDERS
South-East Scotland

Quakers don't regard one particular place as being more holy than another, in one sense (though I'd like to qualify that in a moment).

Our meetings for worship can be held anywhere. For instance, at the moment, in East Lothian they've been happening in people's houses, although the group have recently decided to meet also in converted stables at the back of a manse.

It's even possible to have meetings for worship in prison – I remember one place here where there was a roof but no walls. There isn't any special place which we feel we have to make sacred in order to worship there.

Sometimes in Edinburgh I have a strong sense of the presence of God; sometimes not. I think the opposite of what I was saying before is also true.

Quakers feel that every place can be holy and that God is there when you're doing the washing-up (not just in church); when you're at your lowest, God is there. As somebody said, 'When you're in a hole, God's in a hole too'.

I think we've moved away from the hierarchical God up there and us down here. We try to integrate the spiritual and secular parts of life and not make an artificial distinction.

It is, however, very important that we shouldn't separate the theory, the expectation, the questions of worship and the Church's religious activities from the rest of our lives.

That is the message that is important for Edinburgh, as for other places today.

Quakers also believe that we don't need an intermediary. We may all of us need help – we do – but we don't need a priest to stand there to mediate God for us. God, or the Holy Spirit, or the Great Spirit (or however one may like to define or use the term), is always available and it really depends on people opening themselves to the Spirit, rather than going to a certain place or going through particular rituals and having God brought to them through the rituals and the various actions within the service.

We feel that the big message of Quakerism (which has been here since the 1600s) is that God is available to anybody who really wants to see him.

The Quaker service is based on silence. You wouldn't think it sometimes if you go to a large meeting – but it is. You can have a whole hour without any speaking.

More usually, perhaps two, three or four people may feel strongly drawn to contribute. It's not something that they've brought from what they've prepared beforehand; it's not a discussion. It's something arising from the fact that 'two or three are gathered together in My name'.

Silence is a problem for some people. When you go to a church in other denominations and they call for silence, you're lucky to get ten seconds. So I assume that for some, it's a problem.

It's the unfamiliarity of sitting down together and nobody actually gets going, nobody starts you off, nobody starts the first hymn.

Many people are very happy to have the time, perhaps just once a week, to lay down the burdens. They know they've got to pick them up again, generally. But they can just be quiet and not have to follow set patterns nor be over-influenced by what everybody else is doing. One person may be thinking particularly of one member of the group; somebody may be concerned about the state of the world in some aspects; somebody else may be crashed out and exhausted. Often the young parents, for instance, have been up all night with the kids.

All of it can just be laid down with silence and it doesn't demand that all of us say it all or add it all into our brains. It does leave time for a joint worship to grow up which includes all that, but doesn't get dominated by it.

That's ideally, of course. As with all these democratic processes, they can go horribly wrong.

Western civilisation went to Africa feeling shocked at these dreadful savages and their practices of polygamy and not wearing many clothes. What we've lost is the exchange.

Of course, we've brought things to Africa, although it was all too often linked to economic exploitation and slavery.

But we didn't take the gifts of Africa. Amongst the many gifts of Africa – we lived there for nine years altogether – are friendship, a welcome, a smile. When we first came back, we couldn't believe it – everybody, as the bus came from the airport, everybody was frowning; we only saw that because we'd been living in Africa.

Most important of all, there are hundreds

and thousands of different Africans. Some of their societies have very highly-developed communities with very strong religious beliefs, with very effective ways of appointing leaders (but getting rid of them if they don't do the job properly) and of looking at life as a whole, rather than split up in pieces as we see it.

The very first time I came to Edinburgh I was deeply shocked by the poverty. The Queen and the Duke of Edinburgh happened to be in the city and I was here as a forestry student, just for the weekend.

I walked down the Royal Mile and was quite appalled by the squalor as it then was. It's all beautiful wynds and courts now, but it was extremely poor housing at that time, in bad disrepair and an obvious source of misery for the people there. I thought to myself, 'Why does the Queen have it called "The Royal Mile"'?

Of course we've now pushed this off to other places further from the city centres. But it's not gone away, and the recession and the policies that have been pursued in relation to it have made things very hard.

It tends to be the poor that suffer the most. But how many people from all walks of life have lost their jobs?

Homelessness was one of the matters we raised with our local MP. Quakers have a strong social witness.

We have had meetings with our MP twice now. The first time we raised issues about our worries over the Trident submarine and its nuclear weapons. We missed opportunities in relation to the break-up of the Soviet Union and the Warsaw Pact. This time we talked about homelessness and water privatisation, which was worrying people.

Because Quakers believe that there is God
in every man, it follows that every man is my
brother (if you can avoid the masculine impli-
cations of the word 'brother').

I see the two as part and parcel of each
other; there isn't any point in having a wonderful set of theories or beliefs if you're not
trying to carry them out. You don't always
succeed, but the main thing is that you try.

People nowadays are under such an
enormous number of pressures. Some of these
pressures, like homelessness, are very close;
some of them are in the mind – the worry
that they might become jobless or homeless.
People need support and friendship and caring
more than ever before.

There are a lot of big problems in the
world which we now hear about. This is good
in one way, but it puts extra pressure on
people.

If you really think about nuclear weapons
(even in the somewhat reduced form in which
they now exist), a rational person would go
mad. The destructive power affecting people,
the environment, property, our way of life
and our history and our culture, is so awful
and so huge (almost unbelievably huge), that
people must have been mad to have thought
that this would protect them.

Yet they did. What it means is that all
the time, ordinary people have to say 'No';
they have to say, 'There must be another way'
– not just about nuclear weapons, but about
many other things.

What we actually see is that people are
battered and apathetic and feel they can't do
anything. What we need is a truly religious
activity which speaks out and says 'No';
which helps to bind up the wounds of war

and violence and destruction; which seeks to mediate between people who are opposed and fighting, both within our own city and in our country and Europe and the world; on which one tries to build a better way.

I don't mean that to sound idealistic, because idealism (in the sense of a theory with no practice attached to it) is worse than useless – but a goal towards which people take a small step whenever they can.

EPISCOPALIANS

Revd Alan Moses
FORMER RECTOR
Old St Paul's Episcopal Church,
Edinburgh

The Ark (which has been described as a 'restaurant of the heart'), is our cafe and drop-in centre in New Street. It caters for people who are at the bottom of the social pile and probably even at the bottom of the under-class which exists in most cities nowadays. Large cities have always had these people because cities provide some kind of minimum facilities for people who are homeless, out of a job and probably addicted to alcohol or drugs.

I suppose, in our Episcopal tradition, we would see that as one of the forms of the presence of God, building on St Matthew's Gospel – Jesus talking about 'if you did it to the least of my brethren, you did it to me'.

Our tradition tries to combine a very strong sense of the sacramental presence of God in worship (in the Eucharist) with a strong sense of his presence in the poor and the needy. So that Jesus comes to us as much in the person who rings the doorbell here, wanting tea and sandwiches; comes to our cafe-restaurant place, the Ark; or sleeps outside the church walls, wrapped up in blankets. While it's relatively easy to cope with the God who comes in nice orderly, 'churchy' ways, it's much harder work coping with him when he comes in dirtier, smellier, unpleasant, often quite violent ways.

Many of the people with whom we now have to deal are really quite seriously, psychiatrically ill. This is what the government cares to call 'Care in the Community'. We find that the city centre is a mecca for large numbers of people who have been turned out of mental hospitals. Many are really quite unstable and potentially dangerous.

There is an ironic contrast between the tourist trade, the heritage industry view of the Royal Mile, and its less acceptable underside which, on occasions, is carefully tidied away.

One tends to encourage the other, in that tourists are a soft touch for beggars, and so people who have no other means of income can do quite nicely out of begging at the height of the tourist season. That's become one of Edinburgh's little growth industries in recent years.

We're in a city centre church, in an area which has been depopulated to a large extent over the last forty or fifty years as the slum housing in this district was cleared.

I know, for example, that here in the 1930s they'd probably have a couple of thousand parishioners, and St Patrick's in the Cowgate three times as much as that. Now both of us are shadows of what we once were.

What we have found is that the Church here (while it still has a remnant of people from that kind of community), has developed a new role as a spiritual centre for people who are in many ways searching for God. They find the ideologies or the thought-worlds in which they grew up (which might well have been fairly negative about religion) no longer satisfying.

Somebody who came to see me last year, who had been a fairly extreme Marxist-feminist for 20 years (for most of her adult life), is now a regular communicant, much to her surprise. In her case it was a coming-back to a faith she had abandoned in her teenage years.

We do experience that quite a lot of people (I think that's true at St Giles, for example, and in some of the churches of the more evangelical tradition) come in search of something that they don't find elsewhere.

Many of the people are coming in search of faith, belief, experience of God; are coming in ways which are quite open-minded, questioning, seeking ways forward in life (and the meaning of life) in a way which doesn't allow them simply to rest content with set answers which the Church gives them.

Of course, there are those for whom the Church is a purveyor of security and there are those who need that. We probably all need it at some stage. We all need pain-killers from time to time.

One hopes that the Church doesn't simply become a dispenser of analgesics to keep the pain at bay.

For a city-centre church, which has a lot of people of that kind who are searching, it's quite important to have our feet firmly on the ground amidst the homeless and the alcoholics and the prostitutes, otherwise it can become a rather intellectual exercise, an aesthetic exercise. If you happen to provide beautiful liturgy and music, that can become rather ethereal, unrooted and, in that sense, a rather unsacramental form of worship.

But potentially the use of ritual, ceremony, music and arts and the senses, speaks of the

God who makes himself known in his creation and through his creation – the word becoming flesh; the Creator in an age when we seem bent on destroying his creation, one way or another. It's important to have a form of religion which speaks of it as just that – as the creation of God, rather than simply an accident.

As for the New Age movement, I'm rather ambivalent about it. One Christian response is to be very hostile and negative. In a way, as someone who grew up in the 1960s, a lot of it is the 1960s revisited – there's very little in it which was not around in the age of 'flower-power'. A lot of it is a kind of rag-bag of unconnected ideas, some of which are potentially ways into an understanding of Christian faith and some of which raise questions about neglected areas of Christian faith – for example, Creation.

At least some of the people who come to us on their journey have been influenced in some way or other by New Age thought and therefore it has been a way forward for them.

It's not clear how long it will endure, in fact, because its internal contradictions may well become more obvious as time goes on.

I would take the line that it's far more important to affirm the positive things that people believe in, than spend too much time condemning everything that they may have latched onto on the way, given that largely they've come from a position of ignorance of spiritual and theological matters in the first place.

Faith in Christ is something which can't simply be negotiated away in the attempt to find some sort of 'world religion' which would satisfy everybody. That isn't really a possibility.

The holding of a fairly traditional faith can make you defensive ('There's nothing we can talk about – and you're going to burn in Hell, anyway'), or it can also give you a confidence which allows you to be a bit more relaxed in relationships with others who do not hold it and see that the Spirit may be working in them. An orthodox Christian faith can help you to understand that the Spirit of God is not confined to the boundaries of the Church or any particular denomination in it.

Nowadays one of the things I notice is that there are whole generations who have little acquaintance with any form of religion. I see this with schoolchildren, and in wedding or funeral congregations who know no hymns, know no prayers.

When you say (as clerics do), 'Let's now say the Lord's Prayer', and most of them don't know it – that is a problem; although, interestingly, the Christian religion in particular is far more a news item now than when I was growing up. Then, religion may have been more part of the furniture and was regarded universally as fairly boring.

Today, religion is front-page news.

Religion is still there for many people, but there is a deeply-ingrained prejudice, an assumption, that Religion has been outmoded by Science, is passive and doesn't meet the questions of the age. Popular culture is fairly firmly anti-religious, although folk-religion seems to be entrenched in society in all sorts of bizarre ways.

I was preaching about Hallowe'en the other day, because I had got so fed up with evangelical and charismatic Christians trying to stop children going to Hallowe'en parties. I take a wobbly line on this: I've always allowed my children to go to them.

My children, if they ever believed in witches, stopped doing so at the same time they realised I was Santa Claus. The idea that these two left-wing teenagers are going to start believing in the Devil because they once went to Hallowe'en parties, is just so dotty as to be laughable.

It is not my job to decide what the score-line between good and evil is, but there is a good deal wrong with a society which has places like Muirhouse and Craigmillar and Wester Hailes and seems incapable of doing anything about it.

There's a good deal wrong in a society where large numbers of young people seem to be growing up with no moral standards at all. There are now whole generations of children who have little idea of right or wrong. They've had little sense of the religious dimension presented to them.

In the name of free choice and free thought they've in fact been given only a very narrow presentation of what life is about. They have been given very little to reject and to revalue later on.

I would question young people as to whether the meaning of life is actually to be found in much of what has been proclaimed over the last fifteen years as success and fulfilment. There has been a considerable loss, not only in the Church but in society at large, of a sense of *vocation* as being central to the meaning of human life.

I see the crucified Christ in terms of those who are physically and mentally suffering. I also see him in terms of lots of people with rather sad and wasted lives, who are not going anywhere. They're quite comfortable. They get a reasonable pay-cheque every month or week. In that sense they're not like the people who ring my doorbell at two o'clock in the morning, who have got nowhere to stay. But in many ways the former are unfulfilled.

There's certainly a developing under-class who don't work. That's particularly true of housing-scheme areas.

I grew up in what used to be called 'the respectable working-class' in the North of England. That's a segment of society which has been to a considerable extent destroyed by social and economic change and deliberate government policy (one suspects).

Edinburgh is a very socially-stratified city. You notice this with schooling. The gradations of where you went to school are really quite important in this city. That does affect people's views of society.

I don't know if the city is any more spiritually sick than any other city. There are spiritual campaigns which see Edinburgh very much as a battleground between God and Satan. Rather like trying to ban Hallowe'en, it frequently misses the point. I was trying to say to people who were at Mass the other Sunday that while Christians are flapping about Hallowe'en, racist violence and anti-semitism is on the rise in Europe and we don't seem to be getting in quite such a sweat about that.

Immigrants and refugees in this country are having petrol poured through their front doors, are being beaten up and murdered. If we put as much energy into stopping that as we appear to be putting into stopping pump-kin lanterns, we might get our priorities more along the right lines.

HEBREW COMMUNITY

Professor Alexander Broadie
PROFESSOR OF LOGIC AND RHETORIC
University of Glasgow

I attended the Royal High School, before
going on to study at Edinburgh University. I
return regularly to worship and to teach Jewish
philosophy at the Edinburgh Synagogue.

I have to make the initial point that, as far
as God is concerned, we have to say exactly
the same thing today about the existence of
God as we've been saying for several thousand
years. The fundamental truths have not
changed at all – all that's changed is the
context within which these truths live and
have their being.

In particular, what we have to do as Orthodox Jews is talk about *Divine Law* (much of
which includes natural law concepts accepted
by human society in general). Divine Law is
the most important factor for us as we are
especially concerned that we should make our
own will coincide as far as possible with God's
will for us.

The way we do this is by living in accordance with Divine Law. The Law doesn't
change, but the specific application of the
Law has got to change because of the different
circumstances within which the Law operates.

There is nothing mechanical whatsoever
about this interaction. In many ways it's

highly inventive. The rabbinic literature is full of works of very considerable brilliance when people have put their minds to problems which have never really arisen before, in order to determine what God's will might be in relation to those particular circumstances which have never operated before.

This arises in all sorts of very modern cases to do with the development of science and technology. One quite spectacular case concerns the field of medical ethics. Such things as organ transplants – when one wants to know whether such a thing as a heart transplant should be considered moral. Would this be in accordance with God's will for us?

Do we have to say, for example, that God gave us a certain nature, that we live according to that nature and we die according to that nature and organ transplants are contrary to nature and we should therefore have nothing at all to do with it? Or should we say something else?

Rabbis have wrestled with this and indeed they've come up with all sorts of most interesting solutions to these very difficult problems in medical ethics, focussing especially on one of the absolutely essential concepts in Jewish ethics – *pikuach nefesh* (the saving of lives), which says, more or less, that in circumstances where life or limb is in danger, then you're permitted to break practically any of the different Commandments for the sake of preserving life and limb.

So that, in so far as a transplant will lead to the saving of a life or the preservation of reasonably comfortable living for a person for whom life would otherwise be an absolute misery, then of course the transplant should go ahead.

That is simply Jewish law based upon the interpretation of God's will for us, which in turn is based upon our understanding of the Commandments.

It's a continually interactive process, and that's where the inventiveness comes in because what we're interacting with is a circumstance which is always changing.

In Edinburgh, with its long medical tradition, medical ethics is highlighted. The preceding minister of the Jewish community, Danny Sinclair, was a postgraduate student at the University of Edinburgh, working in the field of Jewish ethics, with special reference to medical problems. He published a fine book on Jewish medical ethics with Edinburgh University Press a few years ago.

This is an indication of the kind of interest that Jews have, not just in medical problems, but in the way they approach these, by considering them entirely within a religious dimension (which also encompasses the moral dimension) and offering a solution on that basis.

As a Jew I have no problem turning my mind in the direction of God. One of the reasons it's peculiarly easy to do so is that Jewish law enters into all the interstices of human living. In almost any situation that one confronts, one is aware of the Divine constraints upon action in responding to these circumstances.

The Jewish faith is a positive one – it's a faith on behalf of freedom, in more than one sense. One sense is that Judaism makes a strong distinction between freedom on the one hand, and *licence* on the other, and considers that true human freedom is only possible under law.

If you remove all law-like constraints from human beings, then we return to the state of the jungle (or what used to be called 'the state of Nature'.

For Jews it's only under the conditions of law that we can find the kind of civilised living which embodies religious, social, economic and aesthetic values which characterise human free activity.

Judaism stands interestingly in relation to that insight, because Judaism includes a very detailed legal framework; and in so far as law does not enslave, but frees, there are quite especially the possibilities of freedom in living a Jewish life (and we're talking here not just of human law but of Divine Law).

This gives a certain very Jewish conception of freedom in this way: that to be free is to live a godly life. To live a godly life is to live a life under a Law which frees and does not enslave.

God can only be a close and immediate figure, immediately present in different ways. One thing I have to stress is that this present-ness is not a physical presentness. It would be inappropriate to think of God as located at some particular point in space. Judaism is absolutely dead set against *anthropomorphism* (seeing God in a human form, seeing God as there, looking like a human being, talking like a human being).

The language of the Bible is full of that kind of expression, but there is a saying that the Bible 'speaks according to the language of the sons of men'.

In other words, we are spoken to in words that we, the ordinary people, can understand. At the same time, we have got to recognise that this is metaphor and it's allegory, and we have to interpret it as best we can.

When it is said that 'with a mighty hand and an outstretched arm' God does something, we must not suppose that God has a hand and an arm. We must suppose that this is a way of speaking about the exercise of Divine power. We characterise power in terms of a strong fist. God has his own ways of acting and this is a way of talking about it. We're not to understand God's presence in the way that we understand a person's presence (somebody looking like a human being); but on the other hand, we do know what God wants of us, because we do have the Commandments – six hundred and thirteen Commandments of the Pentateuch and also the very extensive development of those Commandments on the basis of rabbinic interpretation of them, which is added to through the generations.

When we perform an act out of respect or love for God's Commandments, out of recognition that this is what God actually wants of us, then we are embodying God's will in our actions. Where God's will is being embodied, there God is in the form of His will.

So if you see someone who is, in biblical terms, 'caring for the widow and the orphan', then that is where God is too because this is what God requires of them. Such an action is an embodiment of the Divine will, and you can't get closer to God than that.

God is not a human person or in any way physical, but one way of getting very close to God is to make what is valuable to God valuable to us as well. This is what it means to have religious values. In Judaism religious values are practical values. It's not just a matter of what you believe about God, you've also got to behave in a certain way. God doesn't just want us to believe, he also wants us to *do*.

The Ten Commandments begin with a verse – 'I am the Lord your God who brought you out of the land of Egypt, out of the house of bondage.' That's a statement which is God's signature to the next nine verses, each of which is one of the Commandments. That first verse tells us something about what we have to believe in.

God is where the people are. There is a most important text in Exodus, where God instructs Moses as regards the building of the tabernacle and the sanctuary. He commands Moses to pass a message on to the Children of Israel – 'Make for me a sanctuary and I will dwell in their midst.'

The rabbinic commentary focusses on the word 'their'. God is saying that he will make a sanctuary, but He will still live among the people – amongst all the people.

You can ask, 'Are there any people in particular among whom God will dwell?' The Law of the Pentateuch and its exposition amongst the Prophets places a tremendous emphasis upon the need to care for the stranger in your midst, to care for the widow, to care for the fatherless. In other words, there is an awareness of people whom we would now regard as the *marginalised* in society. The Prophets are saying that if you turn your back on the marginalised, you turn your back on God.

The fact is that there shouldn't be any marginalised people. This is contrary to the Divine plan. Part of the Divine plan is that there are human beings with a free will who freely must do something about these problems which arise in society.

There is an important rabbinic saying that 'Everything is in the hands of Heaven, except the *fear* (reverence) of Heaven'.

As far as ordinary Nature is concerned, there are things we can do nothing about, they are inexorable. On the other hand, we human beings are free to take on board God's injunctions for us, or to reject them and thereby rebel against God.

A full Jewish life involves active participation in the broader community, in order to make that community as good as possible, enabling as many people as possible to lead a rich, fulfilling and fruitful life.

Poverty, homelessness, Third World debt and famine hurt God. In very many cases we find that the problems actually arise from human malpractice. So often it's not dead matter, Nature or the inexorable law of Nature that we should blame, but human beings who have got us into this mess – and not *innocently* into this mess.

So often the dreadful disasters which have overtaken human beings have been due to grotesque mismanagement of this planet by human beings.

We have to note in that respect the rabbinic interpretation of the very earliest verses in the Book of Genesis which are interpreted in terms of man's (not control or government or dominion over the Earth), but his *stewardship* of the Earth. God hasn't handed all this over to man on a plate so that man can destroy it if he wishes.

SELECT
READING LIST

GENERAL

Alexander, W and L Castell: *Scottish Museums and Galleries – The Guide* (Aberdeen University Press: Aberdeen, 1990).

Fawcett, R: *Scottish Medieval Churches* (HMSO: Edinburgh, 1985).

Fawcett, R: *Scottish Abbeys and Priories* (Batsford: London, 1994).

Historic Scotland: *The Sites to See* (HMSO: Edinburgh, 1995).

Scotland's Churches Scheme: *The Cathedrals, Abbeys and Churches of Scotland* (1995).

EAST LOTHIAN

Ferrier, W: *The North Berwick Story* (Royal Burgh of North Berwick Community Council, 1980).

Gray, F and J Jamieson: *A Short History of Haddington* (East Lothian Antiquarian and Field Naturalist Society, 1944).

McNeill, P: *Tranent and its Surroundings* (John Menzies & Co: Edinburgh, 1883).

McNeill, P: *Prestonpans and its Vicinity* (John Menzies & Co: Edinburgh, 1902).

Miller, J: *History of Dunbar* (James Downie: Dunbar, 1859).

Available from: The Local History Centre
Newton Port
Haddington
East Lothian EH41 3NA
Tel: 01620-823307

EDINBURGH

Dunlop, A I: *The Kirks of Edinburgh* (Scottish Record Society, 1988).

Gray, W: *Historic Churches of Edinburgh* (Moray Press: Edinburgh, 1940).

Hayes, A J: *Edinburgh Methodism* (private pub., 1976).

Lynch, M: *Edinburgh and the Reformation* (John Donald: Edinburgh, 1981).

Phillips, A: *A History of the Origin of the First Jewish Community in Scotland – Edinburgh 1816* (John Donald: Edinburgh, 1979).

Scott-Moncrieff, G: *Catholic Edinburgh* (Catholic Truth Society of Scotland, 1961).

Stothert, J A: *Parochial and Collegiate Antiquities of Edinburgh* (J Marshall: Edinburgh, 1845).

Stothert, J A: *A Guide to the Christian Antiquities of Edinburgh* (Charles Dolman: Edinburgh, 1850).

Available from: The Edinburgh Room (ref. only)
The Scottish Library (lending)
George IV Bridge
Edinburgh EH1 1EG
Tel: 0131-225 5584

MIDLOTHIAN

Carrick, J C: *The Abbey of S. Mary Newbottle* (George Lewis & Co: Selkirk, 1907).

Ferguson, D: *Six Centuries in and around the Church of St Nicholas, Dalkeith* (private publication, 1951).

Lunan, M and N: *A Brief History of the Church in Glencorse* (Glencorse Parish Church, 1985).

Old, M: *Roslin Church Centenary* (private publication, 1981).

Wilson, J: *Lasswade Church. A Fifty Years' Retrospective* (private publication, 1893) (W Pollock Wylie, Glasgow).

Available from: Local Studies Collection
2 Clerk Street
Loanhead
Midlothian EH20 9DR
Tel: 0131-440 2210

WEST LOTHIAN

Beaton, G T: *The Knights Hospitallers in Scotland* (James Hedderwick & Sons: Glasgow, 1903).

Bisset, A M: *Episodes in West Lothian History*, printed by the *Linlithgowshire Gazette.* Publisher not known, 1927.

Bisset, A M: *The History of Bathgate and District* (West Lothian Printing & Publishing Co: Bathgate, 1906).

Cowan, I: *The Knights of St John of Jerusalem in Scotland* (Scottish History Society, 1983).

Ferguson, J: *Ecclesia Antiqua* (Oliver & Boyd, 1905).

Hendrie, W: *Discovering West Lothian* (John Donald: Edinburgh, 1986).

Hendrie, W: *Linlithgow* (John Donald: Edinburgh, 1989).

Lindsay, I: *St Nicholas Kirk, Strathbrock, Uphall* (1948).

M'Call, H B: *History and the Antiquities of the Parish of Mid Calder* (Richard Cameron, 1894).

Mackay, P R H: *Sanctuary and the Privilege of St John* (West Lothian History & Amenity Society, *c* 1976).

Maitland, J: *Living Stones* (Wild Goose Publications 1985).

Available from: Local Studies Department
Library Headquarters
Marjoribanks Street
Bathgate
West Lothian EH48 1AN
Tel: 01506-652866

OTHER USEFUL ADDRESSES

Cockburn Association
Trunk's Close
55 High Street
Edinburgh EH1 15R
Tel: 0131-557 8686

Edinburgh City Archives
City Chambers
High Street, Edinburgh EH1 1YJ
Tel: 0131-529 4616

Historic Scotland
Longmore House, Salisbury Place
Edinburgh EH9 1SH
Tel: 0131-668 8600

National Gallery of Scotland
The Mound, Edinburgh EH2 2EL
Tel: 0131-556 8921

National Library of Scotland
George IV Bridge, Edinburgh EH1 1EW
Tel: 0131-226 4531

National Monuments
Record of Scotland
(for architecture, archaeology, aerial photos)
Royal Commission on the Ancient and Historical
Monuments of Scotland
John Sinclair House
16 Bernard Terrace
Edinburgh EH8 9NX
Tel: 0131-662 1456

Scottish Catholic Archives
16 Drummond Place, Edinburgh EH3 6PL
Tel: 0131-556 3661

Scotland's Churches Scheme
Gifford Cottage
Main Street, Gifford
East Lothian EH41 4QH
Tel: 01620-810301

Scottish Museums Council
County House
20/22 Torphichen Street
Edinburgh EH3 8JB
Tel: 0131-229 7465

Scottish National Portrait Gallery
1 Queen Street, Edinburgh EH2 1JD
Tel: 0131-556 8921

Scottish Record Office
1 Princes Street
Edinburgh EH1 3YY
Tel: 0131-535 1314